Great Disasters

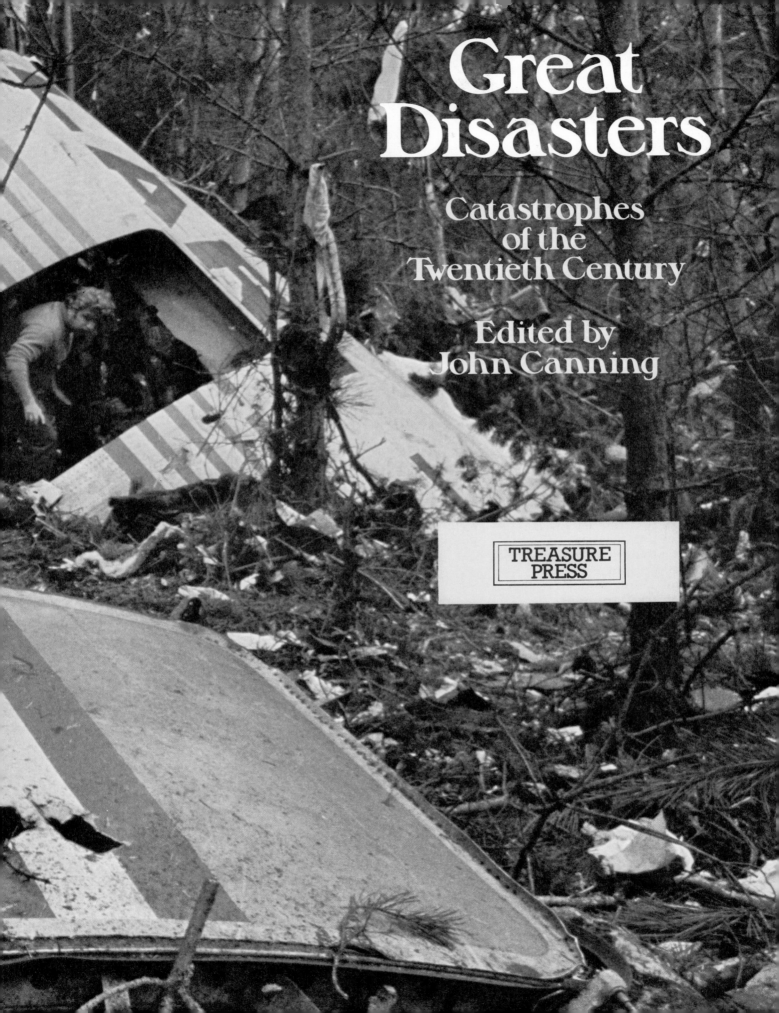

Great Disasters

Catastrophes of the Twentieth Century

Edited by John Canning

TREASURE PRESS

Contents

Introduction

The disasters in this book are of two kinds. The first is the gigantic convulsion of nature: earthquake, volcanic eruption, hurricane, tornado, avalanche and flood. The second exemplifies some of the terrible accidents that have resulted from man's interaction with the highly artificial environment he has himself created: disasters on the railway, down the mine and in the factory, in theatre and club, in ship and submarine, on the race-track, in the air.

We have deliberately excluded atrocities, which presuppose intentional wickedness—man's inhumanity to man. Though probably the cause of more suffering in this century than disasters, they lay outside our purview.

Our presentation has been chronological for disasters do not observe neat classifications and groupings; they occur haphazardly and men learn haphazardly from them.

In each case we have sought to describe and illustrate a very dramatic and tragic event. But in addition we have attempted to look at the causes, and to see if a reduction of risk could be numbered among the consequences.

There is, alas, little that men can do to arrest or mitigate the great eruptions of nature. The San Andreas fault still threatens San Francisco; and Tokyo remains similarly vulnerable, perched as she is on the edge of that great seismic hazard, the Tuscarora Deep. Yet even here something can be done. Continuous monitoring can give advance warning of an earthquake's imminence, and research is active on the unlocking of dangerous faults under strain. Also, as was shown in the Peruvian earthquake of 1970, the better siting and construction of buildings can have a profound influence on the effect of a disaster.

Avalanche protection—prevention and warning—is a highly developed science in Switzerland, and an efficient flood-warning system would have done much to help Florence in 1966.

It is horrifying to think that even when an active volcano was giving alarming indications of imminent eruption, as was Mont Pelée in 1902, the Governor should have stationed troops to stop the citizens of St Pierre from leaving their doomed city. This was a case of human intervention actually ensuring that nature would exact the utmost toll. But in the majority of instances in which men are capable significantly of influencing events—and this applies particularly in the environmental area of his own making—it is not intervention but inertia, ineptitude, carelessness and blind stupidity that are the main causes of disaster.

The circumstances of the fire at the Club Cinq-Sept in 1970 are depressingly similar to those at the Cocoanut Grove a generation earlier. And the same mad behaviour in sections of the crowd during the human stampedes at Ibrox and Burnden Park brought about the same sad results, though the events were separated by 25 years.

Carelessness links the railway accidents at Quintinshill and Lewisham; while structural defects (careless workmanship) probably accounted for the deaths of the submarines *Thresher* and *Thetis*. Massive official inertia was the cause of the Aberfan landslide; and massive official ineptitude the predisposing condition of the Vaiont Dam overflow.

There is a brighter side, however. Slowly and painfully, lessons are learned from bitter experience. Places of entertainment in the United States were made safer as a result of the Iroquois Theatre fire; San Francisco is more earthquake and fire-resistant to-day than it was in 1906; maritime safety was improved as a result of the sinking of the *Titanic*; race-tracks have been redesigned since the Le Mans crash; Quintinshill and Lewisham combined to minimize the element of human vagary in British railway signalling; Aberfan changed the course of tipping policy.

And the brighter side must also include the courage and sublime selflessness with which so many people face or react to the gravest challenge. Even when a disaster seems to be unmitigated, it is perhaps this that saves it from being total.

JOHN CANNING

Half title : Tornado in the American mid-west.

Title spread : Turkish DC10 crash in Ermenonville Forest outside Paris.
Left : Rescue workers amid the rubble of Tokyo after the 1923 earthquake.

First published in Great Britain by Octopus Books Ltd
This edition published by Treasure Press
59 Grosvenor Street
London W1

© 1976 Octopus Books Ltd

ISBN 0 907407 95 1

Printed in Hong Kong

Mont Pelée, 1902

It may not be good for the tourist trade to call some of the Lesser Antilles the Volcanic Caribbees, but that is what they are. Stretching in an arc from the Virgin Islands in the north to Grenada in the south, the Windward and the Leeward Islands have been built up from the ocean floor by volcanic action. On some the volcanoes are extinct, on others, still active. Only two have erupted in historic times, Mont Pelée on Martinique and La Soufrière on St Vincent.

Martinique is now a Department of France, so firmly integrated that when someone says '*Je vais en métropole*' he means he is going to Paris, not Fort de France, the island's capital. But in 1902 the most important commercial centre was St Pierre, a town of 26,000 inhabitants, lying in a mile-long, crescent-shaped strip on the north-west coast, below ravines rising steeply towards Mont Pelée ('bald mountain') which reared, 4,430 feet above sea level, five miles away, almost due north.

Sugar, rum and bananas were the basis of the island's prosperity. St Pierre was a gay town – people called it the Paris of the West Indies – with riotous tropical vegetation, a mixed population of whites, mulattos and blacks, and strongly contrasting wealth and poverty.

Mont Pelée steamed and puffed occasionally, rather like an old man smoking his pipe. The main crater had remained dormant for ages, although there had been a minor eruption in the volcano 50 years earlier. For as long as anyone could remember there had been a lake there called *L'Etang des Palmistes*, and it was a favourite picnic spot. The only other eruption recorded had been in 1792 and that, too, had been insignificant.

On the south side of the mountain, facing St Pierre, there was a dry secondary crater, *L'Etang Sec*, with steep flanks unbroken except at one point, where, also on the south side, a gash in the rim led into a ravine called *La Rivière Blanche* which extended right to the coast. In the rainy season flood water flowing down this and other ravines could cause considerable damage.

On 2 April 1902, fresh steaming vent-holes were noticed in the upper part of *La Rivière Blanche*. Three weeks later, a small amount of volcanic ash floated down on to the streets of St Pierre and there were a few earth tremors, just enough to upset crockery. In the following days the situation became more ominous. There were explosions in the secondary crater which hurled up rocks and clouds of ash. Then a lake formed there, 200 yards across, and also a cinder cone as high as a house, with steam spurting from the top. Soon ash was falling more heavily, mantling and muffling the town, seeping into shops and houses, killing birds and animals and bringing with it the nauseating stench of sulphur. Mrs Prentiss, wife of the American consul, wrote: 'The smell is so strong that horses in the street stop and snort, and some of them drop dead in their harness.'

In response to the considerable alarm caused by these events, Louis Mouttet, Governor of Martinique, ap-pointed a commission to assess the situation and he visited the town. It was the last trip he ever made. Incredibly, the commission reported no immediate danger and while Mouttet maintained a studied air of calm the local newspaper, *Les Colonies*, backed him up with soothing editorials. The extraordinary compla-cency of all three has been ascribed to political collu-sion: important elections were due to be held on 10 May and Mouttet was anxious not to let his supporters disperse.

As ash continued to fall, St Pierre began to look like a body drained of blood. Deep rumblings could be heard coming from the belly of the mountain. Despite troops brought in by the Governor, law and order became difficult to maintain. Shops and businesses closed. Terrified villagers from the mountain slopes burst into bars and hotels demanding refuge. From the other end of the town, people were pouring southwards, swelling the population of St Pierre to 30,000. On 5 May came a foretaste of what Pelée could do. The cleft in its side becoming blocked with ash, massive quantities of rain water had collected in *L'Etang Sec*, been heated by volcanic action and now burst out in a seething torrent of boiling mud to hurtle down the mountain side. The tide engulfed a sugar-mill on the coast north of St Pierre, killing over 100 people, then plunged into the sea, causing a huge wave which swamped the lower parts of the town. *Les Colonies* reported 'the entire city afoot' and 'a flood of humanity pouring up from the low point of the anchorage, not knowing where to turn.'

Far worse was to come. On 6 May Pelée's rumblings turned to a steady roar interspersed with explosions which threw up masses of red-hot cinders. And the Governor did something unforgivable: he stationed troops on the roads to stop people leaving the town. *Les Colonies* found a disreputable professor to declare: 'Mont Pelée is no more to be feared than Vesuvius is feared by Naples. Where could one be better off than in St Pierre?' In a proclamation the Mayor gave his sup-port: 'Please allow us to advise you to return to your normal occupations.'

All through Wednesday 7 May the roaring and the explosions continued. Heavy rain sent more torrents of mud down the mountain carrying huge boulders many tons in weight. Mingled with water, the ash gave the town a top-coating of hot sticky paste. There was only one slender ray of hope for the 30,000 residents: La Soufrière on St Vincent was reported to be in eruption. Perhaps that would relieve the pressure.

Thursday dawned clear and sunny. The people glanced apprehensively upwards to Pelée, and were relieved to see only a vapour column of unusual height. At 6.30 a.m. a passenger ship, the S.S. *Roraima*, arrived in port and tied up alongside 17 other vessels. By then the scene was dramatically different. 'For hours before we entered the roadstead,' said Assistant Purser

During the early stages of the eruption of Mont Pelée in Martinique, clouds of red hot cinders filled the sky and the air was full of the stench of sulphur. In nearby St Pierre foot-long violet-headed centipedes and deadly fer de lance snakes invaded the mulatto quarter. The snakes were eventually dispatched by the town's giant street cats. Despite such hazards the 30,000 inhabitants stayed on – indeed were forced to – and all but two of them died in the catastrophic eruption which took place on 8 May, 1902.

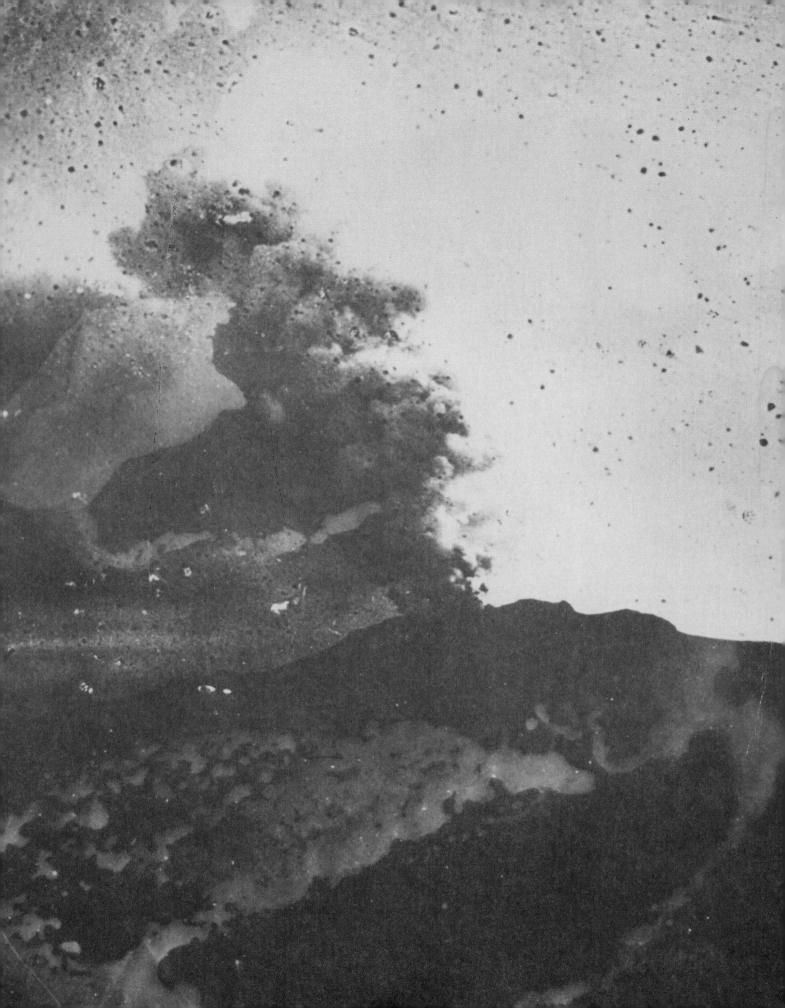

Thompson, 'we could see flames and smoke rising from Mont Pelée. No one on board had any idea of danger. As we approached we could distinguish the rolling and leaping red flames that belched from the mountain in huge volume and gushed high in the sky. Enormous clouds of black smoke hung over the volcano. The flames were then spurting straight up in the air, now and then waving to one side or the other a moment, and again suddenly leaping higher up. There was a constant muffled roar. It was like the biggest oil refinery in the world burning up on the mountain top.'

Thompson thought the spectacle magnificent. Almost everyone on board was watching. There were no premonitions, except perhaps on the part of the Captain, who told a passenger: 'I am not going to stay any longer than I can help'.

But he stayed too long. The mountain-side facing the town was already glowing red-hot and at 7.52 a.m. exactly (the time was recorded on the military hospital clock which somehow escaped destruction) it exploded. 'There was no warning,' wrote Thompson. 'The side of the volcano was ripped out and there hurled towards us a solid wall of flame. It sounded like a thousand cannon. The wave of fire was on us and over us like a lightning flash, a hurricane of fire which rolled in mass straight down on St Pierre and the shipping. The town vanished before our eyes . . .'

In fact there were two explosions, one which shot upwards from the main crater in a dense black cloud pierced with lightning flashes and the other which blew out sideways from L'Etang Sec. Expanding sulphurous gases had shattered lava into fragments and now, through the gaping cleft in the secondary crater, a murderous avalanche of white-hot particles mixed with gas and superheated steam tore down La Rivière Blanche at hurricane speed heading straight for the town.

From its effect on metals it has been calculated that the temperature of the blast was around 1,000°C. People died almost instantaneously wherever they happened to be, with hardly a struggle or a movement, from the inhalation of the fiery gases or from burns, some stripped of all clothing by the blast. Of the entire population of 30,000 only two men survived. Thompson recalled: 'After the explosion not one living being was seen on land.' The town was reduced to a heap of smoking rubble. Walls were torn down, metal roofs ripped off and crumpled like paper, trees stripped to the bare trunks. Within seconds, as the blast passed over, St Pierre reappeared as an ancient ruin, stripped of every mark that had given it identity, like something from pre-history unearthed by archaeologists, though here no digging was necessary. There was no lava crust as at Pompeii, only ash. Searching the ruins later,

Before the eruption of Mont Pelée, the 'bald mountain', St Pierre, lying in a mile-long, crescent-shaped strip on the north-west coast of Martinique, was a lively place with a mixed population of whites, mulattos and blacks and strongly contrasting wealth and poverty among its inhabitants.

rescue workers could barely recognize even well-known streets.

The situation in the harbour was little better. The *nuée ardente*,* or 'glowing cloud' had caused a tidal wave which capsized or badly damaged every ship, and only one managed to escape to St Lucia with 22 of her crew dead or severely burned. 'Wherever the fire struck the sea,' said Thompson, 'the water boiled and sent up great clouds of steam. The blast shrivelled and set fire to everything it touched. Only 25 of those on the *Roraima* out of 68 were left after the first flash. The fire swept off the ship's masts and smoke-stack as if they had been cut by a knife.'

Thompson saved his life by burying himself under bedding in his cabin. The *Roraima* was in no state to put to sea. One passenger who survived, a Barbadian nurse, described how ash poured in through a skylight in 'boiling splashes' as she and their mother were dressing three children for breakfast. The cabin was filling up with the scalding stuff when the first engineer heard their screams and helped them to the forward deck. By then one little boy was dead and a baby was dying. Parts of the ship were on fire and now the whole town was 'one mass of roaring flames'. 'My mistress lay on the deck in a collapsed state. The lady was collected and resigned, handed me some money, told me to take Rita (the surviving child) to her aunt, and sucked a piece of ice before she died.' On other ships the boiling ash stuck to men's clothing, coating them from head to foot and baking them alive. Some were seen crawling about the decks, charred beyond recognition. Many jumped overboard and 'their scorched flesh sizzled as it entered the water'.

One of the two survivors in St Pierre was a Negro shoemaker, Léon Compère-Léandre, aged 28. He was sitting on his doorstep when disaster struck. 'All of a sudden I felt a terrible wind blowing, the earth began to tremble and the sky suddenly became dark. I turned to go into the house, made with great difficulty the three or four steps that separated me from my room, and felt my arms and legs burning, also my body. I collapsed over a table'. Others came into the room, 'crying and writhing with pain, although their clothes showed no sign of having been touched by flame'. Very soon all were dead, also an old man that Léandre found in the house. 'He was purple and inflated, but the clothing was intact. . . . Crazed and almost overcome, I threw myself on a bed, inert and awaiting death. My senses returned to me in perhaps an hour, when I saw that the roof was on fire.' Léandre owed his life to an incredible fluke. Out of all those people, for reasons which will never be known, his lungs escaped fatal damage.

The other survivor was Auguste Ciparis, a 25-year-old Negro stevedore, who was due to be hanged for murder. He was lodged in a structure almost certainly unique in the entire town, a condemned cell, reminiscent of the modern Nissen hut, in the shape of a bisected circle, resting against the outer wall of the local prison. At the front was an aperture blocked by a solid door so low that it could only be entered on all-fours. Above it was a small, heavily grated window.

*Since 1902 volcanologists have used this expression to describe the Pelean type of eruption, which had never been seen before.

Once known as the Paris of the West Indies, this is all that remained of St Pierre after Mont Pelée exploded into a solid wall of flame which rolled over the city. A searing wave of heat killed thousands instantaneously and within seconds St Pierre reappeared stripped of every landmark, as though it were an ancient ruin that had recently been excavated by archaeologists. When, three days later, rescue workers were able to enter the silent city they could barely recognize even well-known streets.

Massively constructed to prevent prisoners getting out, the cell protected Ciparis from the full blast.

Dressed in shirt, trousers and hat, he was waiting for his breakfast when the window suddenly darkened and he was struck by searing heat. At the same moment there was a resounding crash as the prison wall collapsed on the roof. Then, as ash blocked out the window entirely, Ciparis found himself in total darkness. 'I smelled nothing but my own body burning,' he said later. 'Soon I heard nothing but my own unanswered cries for help.'

Three days later, when the town could be entered by rescuers, Ciparis was released, horribly burnt but coherent. He was reprieved, with a suspended sentence, and lived until 1929, earning a living as a side-show attraction in a circus: the Prisoner of St Pierre, complete with a replica of his cell.

On 20 May 1902, another eruption of Pelée combined with an earthquake drove many people from Martinique for ever: 2,000 were killed and several villages destroyed. More violent eruptions occurred on 26 May, 6 June, 9 July, and 30 August. There was a pause until September 1929, when once again the terrible *nuée ardente* roared down, with its super-heated steam, gases and incandescent particles, and tore up the modest structures of a new town which 1,000 intrepid citizens had struggled to build. This time Pelée was too late to catch a living soul: the inhabitants had read the signs and had gone. And this time no Governor tried to stop them.

The Iroquois Theatre, Chicago, 1903

Fire is one of the most terrifying elements. It is accompanied or preceded by smoke which kills more quickly than the fire itself, which travels so swiftly that its victims often have very little chance of escape. When, on 30 December 1903, fire broke out in the Iroquois Theatre in Chicago, nearly 200 people died of the smoke and flames *within 10 minutes*. In the ensuing panic some 400 more were crushed and trampled to death.

It was the pantomime season and one of the first big Drury Lane pantomimes to be imported from England was playing at the Iroquois Theatre, a palace of marble and plate-glass, plush and gilt, with a huge promenade foyer, vast grand staircase and commodious dressing-rooms. It had been opened not long before and was regarded as the last word in efficient theatrical design, convenient, elegant – and safe. The pantomime, *Mr Bluebeard*, had drawn a record crowd to the cut-price matinee, and the theatre contained over 1,700 people according to the management, although witnesses said later that there were many more people standing than the regulations allowed, and the total was probably nearer 2,000.

By 3.15 p.m. the performance was in full swing and the 400 performers, stage-hands and other back-stage workers were fully engrossed in their tasks. A double octet was on stage singing 'In the Pale Moonlight'; the moonlight effect was achieved by the use of gauze draperies and drops and by arc-lamps giving out strong blue light.

It was almost certainly one of these lights – overloaded to obtain the desired effect – which overheated and set on fire the gauzy drapery to the right of the stage which suddenly burst into flame. At once a couple of stage-hands tried to extinguish it, but the equipment available to them was woefully inadequate. One tried to beat out the flames, but the burning fabric was just out of his reach. Then he got a fire-extinguisher which consisted of a small tin tube of powder and tried to throw the contents on to the blaze, with no effect whatsoever. Later, it was said that no kind of proper chemical fire-extinguisher had ever been seen in the stage area.

The flames began to spread among the closely packed drops which were made of canvas, painted with oils. It was ideal fuel and within a minute the fire was out of control; fire hoses were needed and there was not even a fire-alarm located in or near the theatre. A stage-hand had to run several blocks to raise the alarm.

Meanwhile those members of the audience who were seated on the side opposite to the blaze, and especially those near the stage, could see what was happening and began to get frightened. The auditorium was packed with women and children, parties of students and teachers, and girls in their teens. As the alarm grew someone cried 'Fire!' and the audience began to panic; the flames could be seen spreading through all the borders on one side of the stage and up into the flies. The band continued to play and the stage-hands began to lower the asbestos curtain which would cut the fire off from the auditorium.

But two-thirds of the way down it stopped, one end higher than the other, caught on a wire. The stage-hands struggled frantically to free the curtain or cut the wire, but the fire began to billow round the edges of the curtain as a strong draught, coming from a stage-door left open by the fleeing company, bellied the slack of the curtain out into the auditorium.

In the upper tiers the panic was now complete and the audience began to stampede for the exits. The orchestra abandoned its efforts, and when from the stage there came a sudden blast of fire, fed by the draught, which shot an engulfing tongue of flame into the audience, stark terror reigned.

Now every one of the 2,000 people in the building had only one thought – to save themselves. The actors and the stage employees nearly all escaped, saved by the failure of the asbestos curtain, which diverted the fire into the auditorium.

For the hundreds of people in the auditorium there was no such easy route. As the last of the ropes holding up the scenery drops was burned through, a vast mass of blazing material fell to the stage and another great balloon of flame leaped out, and the lights went out.

The scene in the theatre would have defied the imagination of a Dante. People rushed to the obvious exits. There were, in fact, 30, but few of them were marked. Many had heavy curtains over the doors and others were fastened by levers which nobody could work. On the landings, exit-gates were locked and chained to prevent people from the balcony getting down to the circle. On the balconies the aisles were too narrow and the exits too complicated to allow the people to pass easily.

Fire-escapes ran down the wall of the theatre into a side alley-way. When the exit-doors leading to them were finally burst open, the crowd stampeded out on to the ladders, which were totally inadequate for the number of people. Some fell or jumped over the side of the fire-escapes. Most died, and the few survivors owed their lives to the fact that their fall was cushioned by the bodies of those who had gone before. In one angle of the stair dozens died, crushed by the weight of people surging behind them.

One fire-escape from the balcony exit was made impassable by flames leaping from the exit below. Men in a building on the other side of the alley-way pushed planks across the narrow gap, and 12 people managed to crawl to safety. A crowd of women and children awaiting their turn on the iron platform were too late: the flames caught them before they could escape.

The greatest loss of life occurred inside the building, and once again most of the victims had been crushed or suffocated. At turns in the stairs, bodies were piled high. Occasionally someone was found by firemen alive, but terribly injured, among the bodies. On the dead faces were the marks of boots and shoes: flesh had been trodden from the bones and clothes torn from the bodies.

The fire department had arrived promptly upon the scene and – apparently heedless of anybody who might still be inside – pumped in gallons of water which extinguished the flames in the auditorium so quickly that only the plush was burned off the seats.

Within 15 minutes of the start of the fire bodies were being laid out on the pavements and every ambulance in the city had been called to the scene to aid the dying and unconscious. The final death-toll was 602.

The horror was not yet ended. Undertakers made all they could out of the disaster, apparently, commented the Mayor, 'immune to human grief'. Some not only raised their prices but held unidentified bodies to ransom. And as the bereaved tried to bury their dead, the authorities began to look for a scapegoat. The Mayor insisted that he had sent several warnings to the manager of the theatre, who had merely shrugged them off. Inspectors, it appeared, had been bought off with bribes as small as free tickets. No fire drill had ever been held, nobody knew where fire-fighting appliances were kept – nor indeed if any existed. The next day all the theatres in Chicago, and in many other cities, were closed in mourning – and in fear.

There was an inspection of theatres throughout the country, and within a matter of days no less than 50 had been closed as being fire hazards. A series of indictments followed – from which the Mayor did not escape – and all those involved were duly punished, where responsibility could be proven in law.

Soon afterwards statutes were passed on the provision of proper fire precautions in places of public entertainment. Punishment for failure to keep to the regulations was increased.

Officials examine the backstage area where the fire began. Overheated arc lights set fire to flimsy drops, and the failure of the safety curtain allowed great balloons of flame to billow out into the auditorium. Back stage the 400-strong cast of the pantomime Mr Bluebeard *were luckier than their audience. All of them contrived to escape, including a flying ballet awaiting its turn in the flies.*

San Francisco, 1906

The sounds preceding an earthquake can be as terrifying as the event itself, particularly when they come to the ears of people dazed with sleep. Sometimes there is a boom like distant gunfire, or a sharp, snapping sound. There may be a rumbling noise like heavy traffic moving over cobbled streets. As they move forward, shock waves oscillate with a pull-and-push motion while others called 'strike waves' mingle with them, throwing off impulses at right angles. The total effect is like a clod of earth being shaken in a sieve.

The citizens of San Francisco heard a low and ominous rumble at twelve and a half minutes past five o'clock on the morning of Wednesday, 18 April 1906. A few seconds later came the first shock. William James (brother of novelist Henry James), was in a hotel bedroom with his wife. As the furniture began to rock and dance he stayed remarkably calm. 'This is an earthquake', he said to his trembling spouse, 'there is no cause for alarm'– and proceeded to dress with careful deliberation. The whole hotel now seemed to be bumping about.

Most of the 340,000 population were not so detached, though they had experienced lesser earthquakes before, the most recent in 1898 and 1900. This one was much more severe, more ruthless. There were three shocks, separated by only a few seconds and the third was by far the heaviest. One city official later reported watching horror-struck as a massive oak wardrobe in his bedroom tipped sideways, backwards and sideways again before being hurled forward and splintering into pieces. A local businessman wrote: 'I was awakened by a very severe shock. The shaking was so violent that it nearly threw me out of bed.' A bookcase was thrown off the wall, everything on tables and the mantelpiece was

Left : An aftermath of an earthquake is the fire which so increases the death roll. This view shows devastation in Market Street.

Above : Another view of Market Street, San Francisco, from the south. The downtown areas of the city suffered the worst damage.

swept off as in a sudden roll at sea and the floor was littered with smashed china and glass.

Another man in a lodging-house bedroom saw chunks of plaster falling from the ceiling. Then through a gap a child's foot appeared. The next moment, the whole building gave a lurch, the gap closed under violent compression and the foot was severed in a gush of blood. At that point the man panicked and jumped through an open window, just in time to escape from the collapsing house.

A few people were out of doors when the earthquake struck. One was the editor of the *San Francisco Examiner*. He had just left his office with some of the staff and was chatting with them on a side-walk when the ground started rocking violently and they were thrown off their feet. All around, buildings were swaying and tipping under the shocks, throwing down showers of glass, bricks and masonry in a cloud of dust. Tram-lines were snapping under the pressure and reared up like thick metal snakes, short-circuiting in blinding sparks as overhead cables fell on them. Ominously the men could smell gas.

Two young men, Fred Walker and his friend Carlos, had arrived in the city that evening for a sight-seeing tour, coming by sea through the Golden Gate, the passage that links the land-locked Bay with the Pacific. (There was no bridge in those days; it was opened in 1937.) They had put up in a good-class hotel in the north-east corner of the oblong peninsula on which the

San Francisco's newly built City Hall, the pride of its citizens, was said to be indestructible. In fact the dome of its steel-framed tower was virtually the only part of the building to survive.

18

city stands, not far from the area known as Chinatown, then as now the biggest Chinese settlement outside the Orient.

They were not guidebook tourists and knew practically nothing about the city. Otherwise they might have chosen North Beach, known as the Barbary Coast, notorious for its vice and crime, or the Latin Quarter, one of many foreign settlements which included Japanese, Spaniards, Portuguese, Irish, Italians; or taken a look at Nob Hill, aptly named, where fabulously wealthy tycoons, nourished on the gold of the 1840s, the West Nevada silver strike of the '50s, the railroad bonanza of the 60s, held state in grotesquely opulent mansions, one with a $30,000 fence of solid brass which had to be polished every day. Below, stretching south, were the downtown areas with clusters of small houses, built mostly of wood.

If the next day had not brought a different scene, the young men might have noted the city's breathtakingly beautiful setting on its hilly strip of land bounded on three sides by water, met some of its robust, independent-minded citizens, and seen one thing more which summed up San Francisco's flamboyant optimism: the $7,000,000 Palace Hotel. Enrico Caruso had arrived to sing with the Metropolitan Opera in *Carmen* and was staying there that night.

Fred and Carlos felt drawn to Chinatown. Its opium dens, gaming saloons, twisting alleys, and grubby, vicious, colourful life drew them like a magnet and they explored it for hours, until nearly 5.00 a.m.

Twelve minutes later, as they were walking back to their hotel, came the rumbling sounds, then the first shock. Fred was thrown against a wall, while buildings all around began to heave. As terrified people in their night clothes rushed screaming into the streets the two hurried on and found their hotel had become a

Left: Nature makes no distinction between rich and poor. This view from the south of Nob Hill, over a waste of destruction, indicates that it was the more modern buildings in the city centre which suffered least from the devastation. In other parts of the city, where the fires had got out of control, houses were dynamited in an attempt to stop the advance of the flames. But the explosive charges, laid by inexperienced hands were often too large, and buildings blew outwards, starting new fires.

Of all the great mansions on Nob Hill, home of millionaires, only the walls of the great Flood family house suffered little damage. Like many other mansions, however, its interior was burned out. Outside the house statuary still stands on the pavement.

pile of rubble with no sign of a single survivor.

While the Palace Hotel was rocking Caruso is said to have sung a few notes through an open window to make sure he had not lost his voice. Then he went out and sat on his suitcase in the street until someone took him to another hotel. There, pampered but resolute, he swore never to come back to San Francisco. He never did.

Meanwhile, the shocks had toppled some of the fine mansions and left others leaning at an angle of 15 degrees from the vertical. Most of the buildings in Market Street, bisecting the wealthy north from the poorer south part of the city, had been shaken to pieces as well as, except for its massive domed tower, the huge City Hall, only recently completed and supposed to be shock-proof. Elsewhere in the smart quarter a hotel in Valencia Street had gently subsided like a deflating balloon, ending up with the fourth floor at ground level from which the people emerged unharmed.

The worst damage from earthquake alone was in the downtown area, near the site of the original Spanish settlement, Mission Dolores. But loss of life was comparatively small and within a couple of hours many citizens could be seen with utensils salvaged from their shattered homes cheerfully cooking breakfast in the streets. Things could have been worse, they were saying.

Then came the fire. Throughout the city, fires started in dozens of different places, in abandoned buildings from heaters left burning, from hearths, kitchen-ranges, or sparked by electricity or the ignition of gas escaping from broken mains. One housewife struck a match in what had been her kitchen and caused an explosion which ended in hundreds of houses being burned to the ground.

Months before, Fire Chief Danny Sullivan had warned city officials that his Service might be unable to cope with a serious conflagration. Now his words proved horribly true. For 52 fires there were only 38 horse-drawn fire-engines. Great fissures in the streets had fractured every single water main. Except from artesian wells here and there, or from the sea in fires close to the shore, there was not a drop of water to pour on the blaze.

Fanned and driven forward by a stiff breeze the fires were beginning to coalesce into a single inferno and a refugee described the sight from one of the city's many hills. 'Looking down we saw the great tide of fire roaring in the hollow, burning so steadily yet so fast that it had the effect of immense deliberation; roaring on towards miles of uninhabited dwellings so lately emptied of life that they appeared consciously to await their immolation.' He saw roofs and hilltops standing out starkly against the glare of the flames and 'sparks belching like the spray of bursting seas'.

By noon on that first day the fire was totally out of control. Federal troops summoned by the one telegraph wire still intact were on the way, as were units of the National Guard and 600 helpers from the University of California at Berkeley on the east side of the harbour. On the spot, amid the inferno, only two things could be attempted: to save as many lives as possible and blast a gap in the path of the flames. All that afternoon and through the red-glowing night, as the whole of Chinatown was being reduced to ashes, as well as the Palace Hotel, every house but one on Nob Hill, and thousands of houses, shacks, sheds and shanties in the rest of the city, the Navy ferried streams of refugees across the Bay to Oakland on the eastern shore while volunteers strove desperately to keep embarkation points clear of fire. For many there could be no rescue; they had been burned to death where they lay trapped beneath the rubble of their homes. Eighty died in this way in one hotel. As the flames came closer, one man, who was trapped, persuaded a policeman to shoot him.

Attempts to create fire-breaks by dynamiting build-

ings failed. The explosive charges, laid by inexperienced men, were mostly too heavy, making buildings blow outwards instead of collapsing, so starting new fires. On the morning of the second day, Brigadier Funston, commanding federal troops, wired Washington: 'San Francisco practically destroyed. You cannot send too many tents and rations. 200,000 homeless.'

The fires were still raging when a tide of frantic people who had lost everything they possessed began looting. Mayor Schmitz issued a proclamation: 'The Federal Troops . . . have been authorized by me to KILL any and all persons found engaged in looting or in the commission of any other crime.' At the same time soup-kitchens were started and hordes of refugees were fed. One thing was certain: San Franciscans might die from a bullet, but once over the initial shock would never succumb to despair. Some of the accompanying photographs illustrate the resilience required of most San Franciscans.

Fringe areas of the city were saved, but by the Saturday, when the fires were at last burning themselves out, four square miles had been annihilated: 514 blocks containing 28,000 buildings. 450 people had been killed. Loss from earthquake was assessed later at £7 million; from fire no less than £140 million.

Recovery was a daunting prospect, but led by their level-headed Mayor the citizens rallied extraordinarily, helped by a flood of assistance from outside and also by their innate ruggedness and optimism. Many of them were descended from those tough individualists who had come halfway across the world to take part in the 1848 gold rush. Since then there had been many fires and several earthquakes, but every challenge had been met. Now this new one, great as it was, found them undaunted, their civic pride profoundly touched. Even while the fires were still raging orders were being placed for new tram-lines and other equipment. Within two days enough rail track had been repaired for trains to start taking out people whose homes were in other states. Electricity was restored in two weeks.

Proudly, or arrogantly, according to the point of view, San Francisco calls itself 'the city that knows how', but at least the title is deserved. Within three years, while thousands of the victims awaited resettlement in tented camps, more than a third of the city was rebuilt, not simply as a repetition of the old but on new plans with many buildings made earthquake- and fire-resistant. In 1911 the seal on total recovery was set when Congress approved San Francisco as the location of a world's fair to commemorate the opening of the Panama Canal. As if recovery from disaster was not enough, a 650-acre site was then reclaimed from tidal land stretching down from the Golden Gate, covered with landscaped gardens, pavilions, miniature palaces, and the Panama Pacific International Exposition was opened in February 1915. By the time it closed in December, 19,000,000 people had been through the gates.

Nine years had passed since that afternoon when the *Evening World Herald* of Omaha, Nebraska, had reported: '3.45 p.m. EXTRA. San Francisco wrecked and helpless.' Now every trace of that disaster had been obliterated, every connection except one: the cause. That crack in the earth's crust known as the San Andreas Fault had been the culprit, when movement occurred in the rocks on either side. The fault runs for

600 miles from Cape Mendocino in the north to the Colorado Desert, under the sea west of the Golden Gate and down the centre of the peninsula on which San Francisco stands. Along that whole length shifts in the land mass occur frequently, though none has been as severe as in 1906. They cannot be controlled; the most to be hoped for is that some day they will be predicted with greater accuracy. Meanwhile, San Francisco, one of the world's greatest seaports and trading centres, lives on, with its 2,000,000 inhabitants, beautiful, tough, cosmopolitan, energetic, disaster-prone – the city that has known how to survive.

Looking down upon the remains of a once-proud city is the Fairmount Hotel, badly scorched but not burnt out.

The Titanic, 1912

Even at the outset, the *Titanic*'s maiden voyage was marked by near-tragedy. As the immense 46,329-ton vessel moved majestically from her berth at Southampton, she came abreast of a moored liner, the *New York*. Suddenly there came a number of loud reports as the other's thick mooring-ropes snapped like string, and then the two ships began to be drawn irresistibly together. The *Titanic* was stopped, just in time, the strange 'suction' ceased, and tugs nosed the *New York* back to her berth. An identical situation arose a few minutes later when the *Teutonic* also strained at her ropes and heeled over several degrees until the *Titanic* had slid past.

Then the liner was lifting to the surge of the open sea and her crew relaxed. High on the liner's bridge Captain Edward Smith relaxed with them. Beneath his feet, the deck trembling almost imperceptibly with the thrust of her massive turbines, was the largest, the finest and the safest ship that had ever been built. To guarantee that safety, 15 transverse bulkheads sub-divided her from stem to stern; a double bottom was a further guarantee against accident. She was, in the mind of everyone ashore and afloat, the ultimate – the unsinkable ship.

After a brief call at Cherbourg, the *Titanic* left Queenstown (now Cobh) in Ireland during the evening of Thursday, 11 April 1912 and headed out into the Atlantic and waters which the veteran Captain Smith knew well. She steamed steadily westwards, without further incident; the sea was calm, the weather clear and brilliantly bright but very cold. Indeed, the temperature dropped dramatically during the morning of Sunday, 14 April and radio messages received by the *Titanic*'s Marconi man warned of the danger of icebergs.

The ship continued to race on at full speed, her lights twinkling on the dark still water, her engines thrusting her forward at a steady 22 knots. Then, just before midnight, a look-out suddenly screamed, 'Iceberg right ahead!'

Frantic orders were given which would have swung the liner's bows to port, but it was too late. As they began the swing an immense iceberg scraped along her starboard side then slipped astern into the night. Captain Smith was on the bridge almost before his First Officer Murdoch could ring 'Stop engines!' He ordered all watertight doors to be closed then turned to Fourth Officer Boxhall to order him to take soundings. Even as the young officer turned to go, however, the ship's carpenter arrived on the bridge to report 'She's making water fast'.

The doomed Titanic at the start of her maiden voyage almost experienced a disaster which might have saved her from her fatal end. Here she is seen in near-collision with the New York (two funnels) as she sailed from Southampton.

Those of the passengers still awake were unaware that anything had occurred, for the impact had been slight. Lawrence Beesley, one of the survivors, stated that there was 'no sound of a crash or of anything else; no sense of shock, no jar that felt like one heavy body meeting another . . .'

Up on deck, despite the bitter cold, some energetic passengers were actually having a 'snowball' fight, using the ice that the deadly berg had deposited during the brief encounter, while one, obviously a wag and not wishing to leave the comfort of the lounge, held out his glass and asked a friend to 'see if any ice has come aboard; I would like some for this.'

A few passengers asked stewards why the engines had stopped, and were assured that there was nothing

Above: Captain Edward Smith Commander of the Titanic was a veteran of Atlantic waters. He died with his ship, remaining on the bridge to ensure that all his passengers had followed his order 'Every man for himself!'

Above : Having raced through dangerous, icy waters, the liner Carpathia *reached the scene soon after the* Titanic *sank. Within four hours she had rescued every boatload of survivors. Women passengers of the* Carpathia *at once set about providing care and comfort for the survivors, and sewing and distributing clothes.*

Left : The Titanic *was the last word in luxury. This is the Parisian Café, where passengers met for afternoon tea, or to while away the time with card games.*

wrong. The stewards were acting in good faith – at that moment they truly believed that nothing *was* wrong. Down below, however, it was a different story. The men in the foremost boiler-room found themselves swimming as tons of water began to thrust through a great rent in the ship's side. They managed to struggle into the next boiler-room, and then the next, to reach No. 4 which was nearly amidships but still dry.

Realizing that the damage was severe, Captain Smith went to the radio-room where the two Marconi men Jack Phillips and Harold Bride were now on stand-by, to tell them that the ship had struck an iceberg and he wished them to be ready to send out a distress call.

By the time he had regained the bridge it was obvious that the *Titanic* was slowly sinking. The berg had ripped a jagged gash along the liner's starboard bow for one-third of her length, and the ice-cold Atlantic water was pouring in. At 0025, some 25 minutes after the collision, Captain Smith ordered the boats to be uncovered. Ten minutes later he returned to the radio-room to order the operators to start transmitting, adding grimly: 'It may be your last chance.' Immediately the urgent call was crackling into the night, stating what had happened, giving the ship's call-sign MGY and her position, and asking for immediate help.

It was picked up by two liners, the *Frankfort* and the *Carpathia*, although the captain of the latter twice asked his operator if he had read the message correctly, not believing that the unsinkable *Titanic* could be in such trouble. When reassured that it was, he ordered

his operator to reply that he would be coming to the rescue at full speed, and asked his engineers to give him 'everything that they had'.

Meanwhile the *Titanic*'s stewards were going from cabin to cabin, tapping on doors and almost apologetically asking the occupants to put on warm clothing and go to their boat stations, taking their life-belts with them. Still unaware of the seriousness of the situation, most of the passengers did as they were asked although some refused to leave the warmth of their cabins merely for an unexpected and very inconsiderate drill.

The boats were swung out and the order was passed: 'Women and children only'. At first there was great reluctance to leave the ship for she seemed so safe, so permanent, compared to the frail-looking boats. As Beesley was to state later: 'The sea was as calm as an inland lake save for the gentle swell which could impart no motion to a ship the size of the *Titanic*. To stand on the deck many feet above the water lapping idly against her sides, gave one a sense of wonderful security...'

Everyone was behaving in a calm, almost detached manner. There was none of the panic which was to cause loss of life in other ships under similar circumstances, although a brief and ugly scene among the steerage passengers was quickly quelled by the officers.

At last the boats began to be loaded and then slowly lowered, but not actually dropped into the sea. This was because Captain Smith had been told of the replies to his distress signal, especially that from the *Carpathia* which had stated that she was only 60 miles away and

became wider as her stern lifted, then she tilted to attain an almost vertically upright position and remained thus, motionless. As she swung all her lights were suddenly extinguished and there came a deep rumble as tons of machinery broke loose and fell towards the bows. Then the great liner slid forwards and down, the waters closing over her like a shroud.

Soon after 0400 hours the *Carpathia*, having raced through dangerous waters at (for her) a hitherto unknown speed of 17 knots, arrived on the scene and by 0800 hours had rescued every boatload. With her was the *California*, a liner that had stopped during the night less than 10 miles from the *Titanic* and whose captain was subsequently severely criticized for not observing the stricken vessel's distress rockets.

The whole world was stunned when the final accounting was released. Of the 2,206 people on board, 1,403 were lost, mostly crew and male passengers. Yet out of the greatest sea disaster of all time came good. The inquiry resulted in the formation of the International Ice Patrol and also stricter Board of Trade regulations regarding the provision of sufficient lifeboats to carry everyone on board ships.

Left : A lifeboat rows away from the sinking ship. Ship's musicians played 'Nearer my God to Thee', and male passengers, unable to get into the too-few lifeboats, joined in the singing.

Below : Captain Lord of the SS California *with three other officers. The Captain, whose ship had stopped in the night only ten miles from the* Titanic, *was severely criticized for not noticing her distress rockets.*

would be with them within four hours. But the captain soon realized that his ship was sinking lower with every passing minute, and as her bows went deeper and her stern rose from the water it would be more difficult to lower the boats. Some were still only half-filled, many women refusing to leave their husbands. Mrs Isador Strauss was one, saying firmly, 'Where you go, I go.' They stayed together – and died together.

As the boats splashed down, the strains of 'Nearer my God to Thee' drifted into the night from a group of the ship's musicians who had gathered on deck with their instruments. Some of the male passengers joined in the singing, others stared over the ship's side for a last lingering look at the faces of their loved ones before they became indistinguishable in the darkness. The crews of the boats were mainly stewards and stokers, for every officer and nearly every seaman stayed on board to help those who remained.

Two hours after the liner had been struck Captain Smith ordered 'Abandon ship! Every man for himself!' He remained on his bridge and was never seen again. Despite this order, Phillips and Bride were still transmitting, urging the ships that were straining to their rescue to hurry. Then their power failed and they went on deck.

Those in the lifeboats looked back at the sinking liner. The ship, nearly a sixth of a mile long with four towering funnels and still brilliant with light that gleamed from portholes and saloons, was now down by the bows and sinking slowly but discernibly. The angle

Warnings of icebergs in the area had been received by the Titanic's *Marconi* man. When the iceberg struck the ship the Captain ordered the two radio operators, Jack Phillips and Harold Bride, to stand by. Ten minutes later he returned to the radio room to instruct them to transmit an SOS. Immediately the two men started to send out the urgent message, which was picked up by the Carpathia and the Frankfort. Bride and Phillips continued to urge ships to their rescue as the great liner sank lower into the water, and even after Captain Smith had given the order to abandon ship. Only when the power failed did they go on deck to take their chance in the icy waters. Harold Bride, second radio operator, paid for his courage : he was picked up by the Carpathia, both feet crushed and frost-bitten, and had to be carried ashore when the ship docked.

Senghenydd, 1913 and Gresford, 1934

The middle week of October 1913 was a time of disaster, bringing tragedy by sea, land, beneath the land, and curiously (for this was 1913), by air. This one black week saw an horrific death by fire take hundreds when their ship, the SS *Volturno*, became a beacon blazing in the night; hundreds of miners lost their lives beneath the Welsh soil of Senghenydd; two express trains collided near Liverpool; and Zeppelin L11, the world's largest airship, was destroyed by a fire which caused the deaths of all her crew of 28.

Of these diverse disasters, the worst was that of the Welsh colliery, representing, in terms of loss of life, the most devastating disaster in British mining history. Until that time, the worst had been at the Oaks Colliery, Yorkshire in 1866, which killed 388 men; and the Hulton Colliery, Lancashire, of 1910, in which 344 miners perished. Previously Wales's worst disaster had been at Ebbw Vale, Monmouthshire, in 1878, when 268 men had died. The number of fatalities at the Universal Colliery, Senghenydd near Cardiff, was to top them all.

It occurred on the morning of Tuesday, 14 October 1913 at about 8.20 a.m. At the mine, high above the small town of Senghenydd, the morning shift had been deep down since the change-over at 6.00 a.m., the main shift of the day, with nearly 1,000 men at work. In most of the rows of humble terraced houses, wives were cleaning up after breakfast, their children, scarf-wrapped against the October chill were on their way to school; and other miners, their morning bath and breakfast behind them, were climbing thankfully into bed.

Left and below: In October, 1913, the sound of an explosion sent anxious relatives running to the local pit at Senghenydd. Rescuers found their way barred by fire.

Mining disasters represent tragedy not only through loss of life, but also through hardship. After the explosion at Gresford Colliery, three miles from Wrexham in Wales, the pit was closed for more than seven months. The whole complement of the mine, 1,859 persons employed both above and below ground, were out of work for all this time, and suffered considerable hardships. Among others, the Daily Mirror organized a relief fund, and under its auspices farmers brought food for the stricken families.

Then came the sound that every miner's wife dreads – a loud, muffled explosion from the pit. Within minutes, white-faced women, with shawls thrown hastily over their heads, were running into the streets; children, wise in the ways of collieries from babyhood, turned from school and ran crying back to their homes. Soon a sizeable crowd began to gather at the colliery entrance, women and children mostly, standing quietly, apparently unemotional yet desperately eager for news of what had happened. In the beginning all that was clear was that an explosion had occurred within the Lancaster pit (there were two, the other one was York pit), that a cage had been blown out, and that a banksman had been hurled with it to his death. An ominous column of grey smoke was now pouring from the shaft making everyone present deeply concerned for those below. Mr Shaw, the mine manager, went down at the head of a hastily-collected rescue party to the bottom of the shaft. Some hundred yards along the main haulage road they were met by a wall of fire. Further progress was impossible.

During the morning, rescue brigades poured in from Aberdare, Crumlin and the Rhondda and Rhymney valleys, with ambulance men and Red Cross nurses arriving from all parts of Glamorganshire. The silent crowds stood throughout the long day watching men they knew reporting back to the mine from the other two shifts, to help their comrades. Rescue teams from other mines, strangers perhaps but all brothers in such an emergency, arrived, assembled and then disappeared from sight. There was an occasional stir as black-faced men, reeling with fatigue and hawking up the foul air from their tortured lungs, reappeared and, in some cases, brought back survivors with them.

One survivor, Sydney Gregory, later described how, when working in one part of the mine, he heard two heavy thuds soon after 8.00 a.m. and then smoke started to pour from workings further in. He had a small boy with him from Aber who had only begun working the previous day, and although they were close to each other, the air was suddenly so thick with coal-dust that they lost sight of each other. Gregory groped around until he found the frightened boy's hand and then, speaking encouraging words as he went, led him towards the lift-shaft. As they moved they could hear the crackling of the flames and the sound of falling timber until the foul air and rapidly increasing heat was almost too much for them, but they staggered on until at last they reached the bottom of the shaft. Although they were conscious of rescue teams tramping past them they had to wait for nearly two hours before they were able to gain the fresh air above.

By evening of the following day, bodies were arriving on the surface until 42 had been recovered, a pitifully small proportion of the 400 or so men still trapped below. There were tales of amazing rescues. Some 16 hours after the explosion, a group of 18 men had been brought up. They had been found alive, crouching together in 'a sort of shelter' and had been saved, they said, because they had not received the full force of the blast. A family of three was also saved, George Moore and his two sons, although their horse had been killed.

Crowds had grown even larger by the second day, the black-shawled women standing patiently for hours. Occasionally there was a muffled scream and a rush of other women to comfort someone who had been gently told that her husband, son, brother or father had been brought up, dead.

As the bodies were recovered they were laid in the colliery carpenters' shop which had been turned into a temporary mortuary. One observer said that 'Many of the poor fellows have the appearance of having been overcome by a kind of frozen sleep.' In one part of the mine a rescue team had found a father and his son dead in each other's arms and a figure standing nearby also dead. They had apparently been overcome by the foul air.

By 9 October, six days after the explosion, nearly 400 men were still unaccounted for but all hope for them was abandoned. Senghenydd had the atmosphere of a graveyard; in the part where most of the miners lived, there was hardly one street which did not have houses plunged into sudden mourning. Twenty men were missing from Commercial Street, 31 from Caerphilly

Road. One woman, on the morning of 14 October, had said goodbye to her husband, three brothers and four sons as they set off for the mine together; that night she was alone in a house to which none of them would ever return. Such are the personal tragedies that mere statistics never adequately reveal.

The figures are terribly significant. Of the 940 miners who were underground at the time of the explosion, 439 were killed, a frightening percentage.

*   *   *   *   *

Some 20 years and a World War later, Wales was again stricken by a terrible colliery disaster. It occurred at Gresford Colliery, some three miles from Wrexham, on 23 September 1934 during the Friday/Saturday night shift.

At 3.00 a.m. on the Saturday there was an explosion, and flame-tinted smoke was seen pouring from the shaft. Rescue was impossible, although it did not stop the teams from trying. One of them was led by J. McGurk, who emerged, his face showing white beneath the smudges of smoke and coal-dust to say: 'It is hell let loose and not safe for anyone to be near where the fire is raging. There have been three explosions while I have been down this afternoon. They may become more frequent because of the fire and carbon monoxide which the fire is giving off. That is the risk we cannot run. I have been in 10 explosions and have seen nothing like this. From the road where the fire is raging, for 20 yards the stones are red-hot.'

In addition to the crowd of sad-faced women and children who waited at the pit-head, the disaster brought in reporters from all over North Wales. They were soon involved in a bitter argument, for although some 240 miners' lamps issued earlier from one lamp-room had not been returned, Dyke Dennis, managing director of the company, stated that he understood 102 men were still missing, nine bodies having been recovered. Despite the urgent pleas of the pressmen, no further information was given out until a round robin

Above : Despite desperate attempts made to penetrate the barrier of fire which raged on the main road of the mine, few bodies were recovered.

Below : For 36 hours men strove to save their colleagues, but rescue teams were withdrawn for they too were in danger.

signed by all of them finally forced the colliery officials to admit that the number of dead and missing was around 260, although no names were available.

Desperate attempts were made over the next 36 hours to penetrate the barrier of fire, but all failed. Further explosions made it clear that to proceed would be to risk further loss of life. On the Sunday evening the last of the rescue teams was withdrawn, and at 8.00 p.m. a further statement was handed to the press. It read: 'The attempt to overcome the fire in the main road has gone on ever since yesterday, but in spite of very strenuous efforts, and although some progress has been made in this road, the fire has got further hold on a road to the right, through which it was hoped that access would have been got to any possible survivors ... the management, the representatives of the miners and His Majesty's inspectors have come to the conclusion that no person can possibly be alive in the workings. In these circumstances, and in view of the increasingly grave risk to the men engaged in combating the fire on the main road, it has been decided that it would not be right to continue to expose workers to such a serious risk, and all persons have been withdrawn from the mine.'

Next day, lorries arrived at the pit-head and a grid of stout steel girders was laid across the shaft after which concrete and sand were laid on top, effectively sealing the tomb of some 250 victims (the final number of casualties was 264) over 800 yards below. Thirty hours later, George Brown, a greaser, was working on the seal when a tremendous explosion blew it and Brown high into the air in a welter of broken concrete and twisted beams. He died two hours later in Wrexham Hospital.

The seal was replaced. It was seven months before miners ventured down again: those months were a period of great hardship which represented the loss of employment for the whole complement of the mine – 1,859 persons – both above and below ground.

Quintinshill, 1915

Until 22 May 1915 Quintinshill was an unimportant country signal box near Gretna Junction, just across the Scottish border, 10 miles north of Carlisle. From that date onwards, however, it became famous as the scene of the worst disaster in British railway history.

In those days Gretna Green still held romantic associations with runaway lovers. When the great express trains from London reached Carlisle they were handed over to Caledonian engines for their journey northwards.

On that morning of 22 May the two Scots expresses which had left Euston at 11.45 p.m. and midnight were approaching Carlisle 30 minutes late. Because of this, a north-bound local which normally followed them was dispatched from Carlisle before they arrived – the usual practice when trains from the south were running late, because the local provided a connection for Edinburgh and Glasgow at Beattock for passengers from Moffat. On this occasion it was decided to send the local forward as far as Quintinshill and to shunt it there to allow the expresses to pass. Quintinshill was a 'block post' with lay-by loops on the up and down side.

As the local entered Gretna the signalman's telephone there rang. George Meakin, the signalman on duty at Quintinshill, had been taking the night shift and, although he was due to book off at 6.00 a.m., he was still on duty when the local arrived at 6.30. This was the result of a private arrangement between Meakin and James Tinsley who was working the day shift.

Whenever the local was going to stop at Quintinshill, as on this occasion, the Gretna signalman gave Tinsley the tip-off and he then travelled down on it; meanwhile Meakin would write down all the train movements occurring after 6 a.m. so that Tinsley could later copy them into the Train Register, thus making it seem that he had come on duty at the proper time. It was contrary to regulations that Tinsley should ride on the footplate of the local; it was also against regulations that he should, by a private arrangement, report late for duty.

The local made its way to Quintinshill only to find the loop off the north-bound line filled by a waiting goods train. Into the loop on the south-bound side was slowly running a train of Welsh coal empties. Meakin leaned from his signal-box and waved that he was temporarily switching the local on to the south-bound main line until the north-bound expresses had gone through. Nothing wrong with that decision, provided due precautions were taken . . .

When the train had been switched and was at a standstill, Tinsley and the fireman got down and went to the box. The brakemen from the two goods trains decided to join the party: this was against regulations which were explicit; if the guard, brakeman or fireman of any train had to communicate information to a signal-box, he should do so as concisely as possible, sign the Train Register and go.

Tinsley had brought a morning newspaper with him as usual, and Meakin now handed over to Tinsley and settled down to read the paper. He did not notify anybody that the south-bound main line was occupied by the local. Having taken over, Tinsley dutifully set danger signals on the north-bound track and then began 'cooking' the Register.

The telephone rang and Tinsley was told that the second express, due from Carlisle at 6.05 a.m. but now 30 minutes late, had left and was on its way. He went on writing up the Register but was again interrupted, this time by a bell from Kirkpatrick, the next block post, asking 'line clear' for a south-bound troop-train.

Left : In one of the most tragic rail crashes of all time, involving a crowded troop train, an express and a local, hundreds were killed or injured. Bodies of the victims were laid out in neighbouring fields to wait for medical aid.

Below : The devastating fire, which raged through the coaches and killed so many, was fed by the cylinders beneath the coaches which carried gas for the carriage lights.

Meakin had been warned that this train would be coming through and that was why he had shunted the slow coal empties to one side.

Tinsley accepted the troop-train. The men aboard it were soldiers of the 1st/7th Royal Scots – 15 officers and 470 other ranks (and every one of them glad to see the back of their training camp at Larbert, Stirlingshire). On draft to Gallipoli, they would have left days before if the troopship *Aquitania* had not got stuck in the Mersey mud at Liverpool.

The gas-lit train was packed with the soldiers and their equipment. After the first stop, at Carstairs in Lanarkshire, where – though it was only 5 a.m. – the entire population had turned out to cheer them on their way, most of the men settled down to doze or play cards.

When the bell in Quintinshill announced that the troop-train was entering the section, Tinsley sent his own bell signal to Gretna, which agreed to accept the train. The local which had brought Tinsley to the signal-box in the first place was standing there below him, in full view. But he was half-listening to the chatter of the others and half-worrying about filling up the Register. He reached for the signal-lever controlling the south-bound main line and gave the all-clear.

Now another bell demanded his attention. It announced the second express hurtling north from Gretna. Tinsley accepted it and pulled his down signals.

Both the up and down main lines were now signalled as clear.

At any second during these last fateful minutes there might have been a chance of averting disaster, but already the victims were racing to meet one another . . . The troop-train with its complement of Royal Scots had a clear view down the gently graduated three-mile straight which then began to curve slowly under the bridge near the signal-box. The troop-train had been gathering speed down the steep gradient from Beattock and was doing a good 70 m.p.h.

The signals were clear and visibility was good.

Except for the curve.

The driver and fireman had no cause for alarm. There was an unusual huddle of trains by the signal-box, but obviously they must be standing on the loops. The goods train in the down siding obscured the main line, but once beyond the bridge there should be a clear view again.

The troop-train raced down the slight gradient and under the bridge. There, immediately ahead, was the engine of the local train facing them on their own line. There was no possibility of escape. The two engines met head-on. The impact was heard miles away. Coaches of the troop-train telescoped and were crushed forward. The local train was hurled backwards 40 yards. The tender of the troop-train twisted around pulling the splintering coaches with it and heaping wreckage over the parallel north-bound line. The force of the collision was such that the troop-train's length of 213 yards was reduced to less than 70 yards.

Tinsley and Meakin looked at the spectacle, petrified. Suddenly Meakin screamed, 'Where's the 6.05?' Tinsley seemed frozen to the spot, but Meakin made a dash at the levers to set the signals to danger. He was too late. The second express was already in section. No power on earth could have stopped the express as it hurtled into the wreckage of the first coach. Only a minute separated the two collisions – the troop-train was already ablaze when the express smashed into it. Instantly the two fires fused into a single flaming mass fed by gas cylinders under the carriages which had been charged to a pressure of 80 pounds to the square inch.

A reporter on the scene wrote later: 'When the awful force of the second collision burst upon the troop-train, engines were heaped on one another, carriages telescoped and overturned. Men were pinned helplessly beneath them. The carriage doors were jammed and scarlet flames belched from the blazing interior. As dawn was breaking the bird chorus mingled ghoulishly with screams of human anguish. It was an unbearable experience.'

One doctor, hearing a soldier cry out 'For God's sake get me out!' crawled beneath a blazing carriage on which hoses were playing and amputated the man's leg. From the flaming ruin of another coach someone screamed: 'Shoot me, mate, for God's sake shoot me!'

Messages began to speed across the country. A rescue team was on its way but, incredibly, nobody alerted the fire-brigade, and it was three hours before one arrived from Carlisle. It took a long time to give even an approximate reckoning of casualties in the triple crash. In the express eight people had been killed and 54 injured; two passengers died in the local; the driver and fireman of the troop-train had been killed instantly.

The roll-call of the Royal Scots was a macabre experience: all records were destroyed in the disaster and it was left to the colonel and one surviving sergeant to round up the few dazed survivors and work things out.

Out of 15 officers and 470 men, 227 were dead, 246 injured, many of them seriously.

A week after the catastrophe James Tinsley and George Meakin were taken quietly away to await trial for manslaughter. Asked by officials after the crashes how it could possibly have happened, Tinsley had said: 'I forgot about the local on the up-line.'

The Board of Trade's Inspecting Officer, Lieutenant Colonel Druitt, came to the conclusion that the tragedy was certainly caused by lack of discipline on the part of the two signalmen, Meakin and Tinsley. He felt that the means then provided by the Caledonian Railway for reminding signalmen of any vehicles standing within their control at a place like Quintinshill should have been sufficient – if the signalmen concerned had only observed the ordinary simple rules of block working and the regulations laid down for the purpose.

Tinsley was given a three-year prison sentence and Meakin got 18 months. Not included in the sentences was a lifetime of remembering.

Witnesses arriving for the inquiry into the rail disaster at Quintinshill included those who had themselves suffered in it. The Board of Trade's inspecting officer concluded that the tragedy had been caused by lack of discipline on the part of two signalmen who were on duty at the time, and who had failed to observe simple rules.

The roll-call which revealed the full story. Only 52 men out of almost 500 answered the roll-call which had to be taken after the crash, for all the records of the Royal Scots Regiment had been destroyed. In all, 227 men were killed and 246 injured, many of them seriously.

Tokyo, 1923

On Sunday, 2 September 1923, a news report came via Shanghai from Osaka, Japan. It read: 'Yesterday, Yokohama and most of Tokyo totally destroyed in devastating earthquake followed by fire. Heavy loss of life.'

For some days, because of shattered communications, news of what had happened reached the outside world only in fragments.

On 3 September, more reports trickled through: '100,000 people reported killed, 200,000 buildings destroyed, including all Tokyo's business quarter and most government offices. A power station collapsed, killing 600. Tokyo arsenal exploded. Water system completely destroyed. Food warehouses burned to the ground. Fires still raging.'

On 4 September: 'Casualties mounting, possibly 150,000 killed. Railway station in ruins; Japan's longest tunnel at Sasako caved in, suffocating a trainload of passengers. Sumida River burst its banks, drowning hundreds. All bridges down. Almost all schools, hospitals, factories wrecked. Summer resorts on Sagami Bay (20 miles south-west of Tokyo) obliterated.'

On 5 September: 'Many passenger and goods trains derailed with heavy loss of life. Tidal waves, 40 feet high, swamped Sagami Bay, causing massive destruction, then receded, baring the ocean floor. Oil-storage tanks at Yokohama exploded. 40,000 people burned to death by fire cyclone in Tokyo park. 1,600 crushed, then burned in subsequent fire when Fuji cotton mill collapsed. American hospital thrown bodily with all its inmates from cliffs above Yokohama. Count Yamamoto, recently appointed Prime Minister, was attempting to form a cabinet at Tokyo Naval Club when the floor gave way, killing 20 of his colleagues. Estimated casualties: 500,000 homeless of whom many injured. Total dead, in population of 3,000,000, unknown. 1,500 prisoners released from the Ichigaya prison, Tokyo, when the building was threatened with collapse and more have broken out from other prisons. There is now widespread robbery with violence, looting of abandoned premises, rape and motiveless murder. This has been blamed, apparently unjustly, on several thousand Korean immigrants living in the city and some hundreds have been lynched. Martial law has been declared.'

By 6 September, the London *Times* correspondent reported that Yokohama had been 'wiped off the map'. In Tokyo there were now one and a half million homeless. 'The difficulty of telling such a vast story is to

A plain of black ashes is all that remains of much of Tokyo after the earthquake and fire which destroyed some 334,000 houses.

know where to begin.'

The horror had begun at 10 minutes before noon on the hot, sunlit morning of Saturday when the first earthquake shock, more powerful than any felt in 70 years, struck Tokyo and the port of Yokohama, eight miles to the south-west of the outer fringe of the city on the shore of Tokyo Bay.

The islands of Japan, lying within the south-east Asian seismic belt and perched on the edge of the great Pacific trench known as the Tuscarora Deep, suffered thousands of shocks every year and building methods had been adapted accordingly. In Tokyo in 1923 there were some western-style ferro-concrete buildings linked by broad roads near the centre, but the rest of the city was still one gigantic village with narrow twisting paths running between small, one-storey homes clustered closely together and made in a traditional style of lightweight timber, paper and thatch. The beams in these houses were not nailed but dove-tailed together so that when earth-tremors became heavy the inhabitants could simply dismantle the structure.

But in 1923 disaster was beyond control. In Tokyo, the first shock, followed by two others equally massive, destroyed even newer buildings and left the terrain like a corrugated roof with the raised parts eight or nine feet above the normal level. Huge chasms opened in the streets swallowing up people, even tram-cars, then closing on them like a giant mouth. Telephone wires and overhead electric cables were snapped like string, people tripping over them in their panic being electrocuted; an entire tram-load died in this way, struck rigid, according to an eye-witness, as they had been in their last moment of life. 'We saw them sitting in their seats, all in natural attitudes. One woman's hand was held out with a coin as though she had been on the point of paying her fare.'

The earthquake was not the deadliest killer. Fire, caused largely by exploding gas-mains, destroyed thousands more. Driven by a strong wind the flames were soon roaring through the city. Hordes of terrified

Above : In a city largely in ruins, survivors searched among the rubble for what few possessions might have survived

Right : Tents were set up for the homeless and the military and rescue services distributed food, which often only consisted of a handful of rice.

Japanese talent for creating a botanical paradise.

Yokohama, a modern, struggling port with hardly anything old or picturesque about it, but economically most important, was also struck by the earthquake and fire which occurred almost simultaneously. The first great shock which sent the American hospital and many luxurious homes toppling from The Bluff also buckled the quays into snake-like convolutions, wrecked a long pier stretching out into the Bay, destroyed the customs house at its head, tore chasms in the streets, shattered bridges, demolished the two big hotels burying 180 guests, and ripped open the oil tanks.

As the second and third shocks quickly followed, crowds of terrified people stampeded to the shore expecting to find safety in small boats, only to see a wall of blazing oil spreading inexorably towards them across the water. Many were burned, others rowed frantically towards the *Empress of Australia*, at that moment being drawn by tugs out of the Bay, and ultimately 12,000 were picked up by the liner. 21,000 died in Yokohama that day.

Final estimates of the total dead in both cities were around 150,000, and of the severely injured, 100,000. Apart from larger buildings, some of which had stood up well, 700,000 small homes had been destroyed. No one even tried to assess the financial and economic loss. The rescue services, principally the army, and the survivors themselves fought back strongly. At first, there was only a handful of rice for each person each day, and one correspondent noted that a man he knew to have been 'worth millions' was grateful to get even that. But supplies from outlying districts built up quickly and until the telephone system was restored the army ran a carrier-pigeon service with other cities to make known the local needs. Thousands of the homeless were evacuated; tents were provided for the remainder. Within days some water mains had been repaired and in the following weeks, helped by a government scheme for compensation, many small businessmen were back, setting up shop again.

Massive aid came from many countries, including Britain and the U.S.A., in money, emergency supplies and medical teams, and within seven years Tokyo and Yokohama had been completely rebuilt. By 1930 they were new cities with barely a scar.

Today, having risen once more phoenix-like from their ashes, the capital city and its port are only part of a continuous urban-industrial belt containing the largest concentration of population in Japan. Experts say that even reasonable safety from earthquakes has not yet been achieved – and perhaps it never will be.

people tried to escape into the large grounds surrounding the Imperial Palace, even into canals where they stood for hours, only to be found later dead, their heads charred beyond recognition and the rest of their bodies intact. One woman was lucky: she stood neck-high in water with a baby on her head for a whole day, and both survived. Elsewhere some young girls were found cowering inside a large drain-pipe. Others had thought themselves safe in Tokyo's many parks but freak conditions produced whirling funnels of flame which swept across great distances to snatch hundreds of victims high in the air and fling them incinerated to earth again.

For the first 36 hours, people could do no more than try to survive. Large numbers of troops for clearance work, military engineers and relief supplies were on the way, but help from beyond Japan took time to organize. Meanwhile the fires could not be stopped, even by blowing up buildings in their path, and on the Saturday night, beneath a sky that itself seemed on fire in a dome of scarlet and orange above the stricken city, pathetic groups huddled wherever they could find space to breathe, clutching the few belongings they had managed to salvage. Some wandered about near where their homes had been with the names of missing children, relatives and friends scrawled on bits of paper which they held out to strangers or hung from their necks, because their throats were too parched to be able to speak. On the following night, Sunday, when the fires were dying for lack of fuel, people were seen still searching, groping about with little paper lanterns on poles, their mouths covered against clouds of choking white dust that the wind was whipping across smouldering ruins.

In Yokohama the scene was equally terrifying. Yet the purely physical destruction was not as tragic as in Tokyo which, under its former name of Edo, had been inhabited for 4,000 years and contained many cultural treasures. Seventeen libraries were destroyed in the fire, including that of the Imperial Palace, as well as 151 Shinto shrines, 633 Buddhist temples and many beautiful gardens brought to perfection by that particular

The R101, 1930
and the
Hindenburg, 1937

The R101, *hope of the embryo airship industry, flying over St Paul's Cathedral in London.*

Below: The troubles, both technical and political, that had attended the birth of the R101 *ended in this field in northern France, among the twisted heap of metal which had once been a great airship.*

The airship industry is probably the only industry to die in modern times because of disasters, although it experienced only two, the *R101* and the *Hindenburg*, which had a combined death-toll of less than 100. There have been much worse disasters, on land, at sea and in the air, but none has brought to such an abrupt halt the industry from which it evolved. Perhaps the seeds of disaster lay not in its flying machines, but in the industry itself, with its vulnerable technology resting upon politics.

It was not a young industry: the rigid airship evolved from the non-rigid blimp, and that in turn came from the ordinary balloon. Manned balloons were used by the French more than 200 years ago, and in wartime had obvious reconnaissance functions, but as they were largely at the mercy of the wind it became obvious that an elongated envelope propelled by an engine was essential if such dirigibles were to prove tactically useful.

The first truly successful airship, designed by Frenchman H. Giffard, was steam-powered and could offer a speed of 5 m.p.h. in still air. A more practical electrically-powered machine named *La France* took to the air in 1884. From then on designs improved until, in the period 1910 to World War I, the German Zeppelin pioneered air travel by safely carrying some tens of thousands of passengers over a distance of several million miles.

Although progress was made mainly by Germany and France, Britain had produced a few non-rigid air-ships (the first rigid machine, *The Mayflower*, crashed on its maiden flight). World War I demonstrated the success of the Zeppelin in air raids, but also its weaknesses (in particular the use of hydrogen as a lifting gas as the U.S.A. would not export non-inflammable helium), but it was from a forced-down Zeppelin in 1916 that Britain, copying the basic design, started serious work on its own rigid airships. Meanwhile the much smaller blimp had become fashionable as an observation post, especially for submarine detection. By the end of the war the airship industry had a rather healthy look about it.

By 1919 Britain had built two rigid airships – the *R33* and the *R34*. Defeated Germany was prevented from making any more Zeppelins until 1926, but had nevertheless been studying some of the more sophisticated problems involved.

Then came the two disasters – seven years apart – that virtually put a stop to airship manufacture in every country in the world. In 1930 came the destruction of Britain's *R101* (47 dead) followed, in 1937, by the more dramatically publicized *Hindenburg* disaster (36 dead). Germany kept its *Graf Zeppelin* in passenger service for another year, but World War II was imminent and it was already obvious that the battlefield of the air would in future be dominated by the much faster and more manoeuvrable heavier-than-air machines, and that bombers, as they were made bigger and adapted for troop transport, would form the nucleus of civil aviation to come.

Although the use of airships as a slow-speed form of transportation for heavy freight today has its protagonists, most people regard the 'gasbag' era as dead. The process of dying began with the *R101* and the subsequent breaking-up for scrap of the better-designed *R100*.

In 1924 the British Government decided to stop toying with airships and moved seriously into the industry with the construction of the *R100* and the *R101*. The *R100* would be built by the Airship Guarantee Company, a subsidiary of Vickers at Howden in Yorkshire, while the *R101* was to be manufactured by the Air Ministry itself, at Cardington in Bedfordshire. The *R100*'s builders were short of cash but long on expertise, being able to call on Dr Barnes Wallis of subsequent 'Dam-buster' fame, and many other top-ranking scientists and engineers including Nevile Shute (*No Highway*) Norway, whose first two names became a household word.

The Ministry, however, suffered from lack of designing talent, as many of its experienced men had been killed in the war. It also suffered from over-exposure in the press as, with taxpayers' money involved, every stage in the work at Cardington had to be publicized. Thus, errors which the Airship Guarantee Company was able to rectify in silence had to be retained – for

example, the too-heavy British diesel engines which the A.G.C. quietly swopped for lighter, petrol-driven power units.

Troubles and arguments, both technical and political, ended with the *R101* slower by 10 m.p.h. at 71 m.p.h. and, at 25 tons, with only half the disposable lift of her sister ship. The airship was flown to the Hendon Air Display in the summer of 1930 to let the public admire her, but only experts could have known she was losing gas and that she would only be able to return to Cardington by throwing out huge amounts of ballast. It was there that drastic and, in the event, foolish action was prescribed: instead of taking steps to reduce weight it was decided to increase it by cutting the airship in half, inserting a new metal bay (thus adding to her length) and putting in more bags of hydrogen for lift.

While all this was going on, the privately built *R100* made a very successful flight to Canada. Air Minister Lord Thompson, perhaps somewhat put out, decreed brusquely that *R101* would leave for India via Egypt on 4 October, with himself on board. By then the airship would be 'safe as a house, save for the millionth chance' – and anyway, he had to get back on time for a meeting. This was all very impressive, though it is not known to what extent Thompson's enthusiasm was generally shared.

The largely untested *R101* left its Cardington mast on the ordained date with 54 people aboard, of which only six were passengers. In these days of plastic synthetics it is difficult to realize that the dural frame contained 17 hydrogen-filled gasbags made from the membrane of bullocks' intestines, held in position by hundreds of wires. New valves were fitted to control the gas, but they tended to 'over-react' causing them to release gas at an unexpected air turbulence, thus releasing gas prematurely. This was one of many control problems.

Despite efforts to save overall weight, no limit was placed on personal luggage; Lord Thompson's private effects weighed as much as 24 people. The airship's fittings included silver cutlery, potted palms and 600 feet of heavy Axminster carpeting. Supplies of food and drink were lavish, as there was to be an aerial state banquet over Ismailia, with Egyptian notables and other distinguished figures as guests. Because of the inconvenience of refuelling during a banquet (no smoking, etc.) the ship was carrying nine more tons of diesel oil than she needed to reach her destination.

Small wonder that the *R101* shuddered painfully into the sky that evening. A resident of Hitchin later told the *Daily Express* that she had run out of her house to find everything lit by 'a ghastly red and green light . . . there was the *R101* heading straight for the house . . . she cleared the trees of our drive and the house by the smallest margin . . . as the green and red tail-lights moved away up the drive horror descended on us all.'

A few hours later Le Bourget airport in France confirmed that the airship was one kilometre north of

The vast, burnt-out framework of Britain's R101, in which 47 people died, lies in a field in Beauvais looking like the skeleton of some strange primeval monster.

Right : Only seven crew members survived the crash of the R101 *: one of the injured arriving at Croydon.*

Far right : Passengers of the Hindenburg *were luckier ; 61, out of 97, survived.*

Below right : The great ship was as vulnerable as had been the R101 *: a flash of flame suddenly appeared, and the huge airship was totally burnt out.*

Below : The dining saloon of the Hindenburg.

800 feet, she was the biggest airship ever built. Power came from four mighty Daimler diesel engines driving propellers in separate gondolas under the great gas-lifted hull. As with all airships, the gas was contained in a quantity of separate bags, or cells. Today, these would be made completely gas-tight, but in 1937 a slow seepage was expected and allowed for.

This brought with it the danger of fire, but designers had perfected the interior passenger quarters, with their 25 two-berth cabins, spacious dining-room, saloon and reading-room, so that there was almost no risk of hydrogen entering. Smoking was confined to one absolutely safe room, with double-doors and an ingenious method of keeping its air pressure higher than elsewhere, so that no gas could possibly enter. Passengers could smoke freely here, though the cigarette-lighters were chained to tables to prevent the absent-minded taking them to their bedrooms. (Matches and lighters were totally forbidden to all passengers and crew.)

Elsewhere, in this ingenious, luxurious, ship was a baby grand piano, made of aluminium. On either side

Beauvais. After 2.07 a.m. the *R101* stopped replying to wireless messages, and by 2.08 horrified villagers had been woken by the noise and then the inferno. Le Bourget's operator tapped out the words, '*G-FAAW a pris feu*'.

G-FAAW – *R101* – had indeed caught fire, as a result of not clearing a low hill at Beauvais. It was all over in minutes. Unlike the more fortunate *Hindenburg*, there was no chance for passengers and most of the crew, for they were sleeping. Seven crew members survived.

No one knows for certain why the *R101* hit the ground at Beauvais. Perhaps she broke up under aerodynamic stress, perhaps a gas bag punctured, perhaps she simply lacked sufficient lift. Whatever the cause, it ended Britain's contribution to the development of the airship. *R100* was immediately grounded, then broken up for scrap.

That was almost the death of the airship industry as a whole, but not quite. The Germans continued, and by 1936 had completed the *Hindenburg* to join its sister ship *Graf Zeppelin*. With a length of rather more than

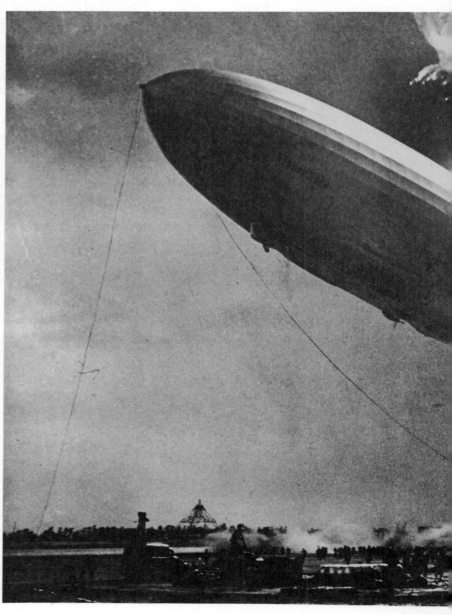

were promenade decks from which passengers could look out and down through big sloping windows.

The *Hindenburg* made a number of flights to the United States and to Brazil during 1936–37, and May 1937 brought yet another scheduled departure from Frankfurt to the American terminus at Lakehurst. Nothing could have been more routine; no German passenger airship or Zeppelin had yet crashed. From those first flights in 1910, many thousands of people had been carried safely to their destinations.

Slowly she rose into Frankfurt's sky on the evening of 3 May. Her passenger accommodation was half empty (though it was almost fully booked for the return trip) and the 36 on board, with a standard crew, totalled 97. Estimated time of arrival at Lakehurst was 8 a.m. on the 6th, but very soon Captain Max Pruss realized that strong headwinds were going to upset the schedule.

It was already 15.30 on the 6th when *Hindenburg* passed over New York's Empire State Building – a regular practice, to advertise Germany and her great airship to the people below, and give passengers an exciting, unfamiliar, look at the city. However, what interest there might have been in the arrival of another airship flight was diminished, rather than heightened, by its lateness. Apart from passengers' friends and relatives, few people were heading for Lakehurst. Hardly any of the press were turning out; one radio company had sent a commentator, Herb Morrison, with a portable recorder.

Bad weather made Pruss delay his arrival still further, and it was not until 7.00 p.m that he began his approach to the Lakehurst mooring-mast.

The first lines were dropped to the ground crew at 7.25 p.m. A slightly bored Herb Morrison began his commentary, unaware that it would become one of the most moving records of human anguish.

There was a flame, and Morrison's voice, abruptly kindling with it to hysteria, sobbed, 'It's broken into flames, it's flashing, flashing, flashing terribly, it's bursting into flames!'

Those inside were the last to know, and to this day no one can be sure what caused that flame. Miraculously, with seven million cubic feet of incandescent hydrogen about them, only 36 died out of *Hindenburg's* airborne total of 97. Much credit for this must go to officers and men at Lakehurst, who risked death to lead shocked, hurt, passengers and crew out of the holocaust.

So ended the day of the passenger airship. The rest of the world, including Britain, which had been watching the Germans with interest, gave up hope that these monsters of the sky would ever be safe and practical. There were undoubtedly other unspoken considerations, for no industry could die with such a small casualty list. The Germans withdrew the perfectly safe *Graf Zeppelin* in 1938, and in retrospect the reason is obvious. Zeppelins were not war machines. Balloons and blimps continued, however, while the real hardware of fighters and bombers took over.

There remains the possible return of the airship for freight transportation. Independent of land or sea it can travel 'as the crow flies', which offers advantages. In the long term, the issue will be decided by sheer economics, for a freight airship must make a profit if it is to survive – or even become a reality.

The Morro Castle, 1934

The *Morro Castle* was a vessel of 11,520 tons, pride of the Ward Line of America, dignified and stately, beautifully furnished and equipped, and only four years old. Although originally designed as a 'ferry' running between New York and Havana, she had become a popular cruising liner for those seeking sun, sea and relaxation and also an escape from the rigours of prohibition of the time. For no illicit speak-easy 'bath-tub' liquor was drunk on board *her*. Everything – spirits, wines and liqueurs – was imported and was the real thing. Consequently the trip to Havana and back was, as many regulars agreed, 'one helluva cruise.'

The final night of each voyage was inevitably the wildest and noisiest of them all with everyone making the most of the last night of riotous freedom before arriving in New York at eight o'clock on the following morning.

Even the repeal of prohibition in the previous year made no difference – the last night in the *Morro Castle* was, by tradition, an abandoned, uninhibited affair and this particular night of Friday 7 September 1934 was no exception. Many of the passengers had been having last-minute parties in their cabins and were arriving in the warm, perfumed and rich-food-scented atmosphere of the main dining-room. Only at the captain's table where a number of the privileged had assembled was there a slight note of discord. The guests were there, but where was their host, Captain Robert Willmott? While they waited, undecided whether to start without him, a page-boy arrived with the captain's apologies – he could not attend for the moment. Actually the popular, English-born captain was already dead from a heart attack and had been found a little earlier by his second-in-command, Chief Officer William Warms, lying slumped, half-dressed, over his bath.

The inevitable rumours began to spread around the room until an officer announced what had happened and that Warms had taken over command of the ship. The sad news effectively ended the evening's festivities. The orchestra left the stand, lights were dimmed and the public rooms slowly emptied, although parties still continued in the cabins. It was said later that several girls had to be carried back, insensible, to their own cabins and that some members of the crew were fired for being drunk.

Up on the bridge, Warms stared into the night, conscious of the responsibility of this, his first command. A strong north-easter was building up, rain was lashing across the decks and vivid lightning was illuminating the dark, churning waves. At 2.00 a.m. the ship altered course for the Ambrose Light and New York harbour and Warms relaxed; another six hours would see the ship at Pier 13 and the present ordeal over.

Then with terrifying suddenness, a report reached the bridge from a night watchman who had seen smoke drifting from a ventilator. An officer sent to investigate returned white-faced and shaken. A fierce fire was already raging in the ship's library and a steward, opening a locker, had staggered back as a great gout of flame leaped from its interior. He had then run to one of the levers which controlled the ship's elaborate fire-control system and pulled, hard. Nothing happened.

From that moment the liner was doomed.

Even as the alarm was being raised, a great mushroom of smoke and flame was rising high above the ship's superstructure, sparks and cinders raining down upon her decks. For the most part the ship's crew was unable to cope with the situation. A good number were stewards – ship-borne waiters – many of whom used the liner as an easy way of life, some even for a little lucrative smuggling on the side, and their first thought was for themselves. It turned out later that in the first six lifeboats, with a total capacity of more than 400, which pulled into Spring Lake, New Jersey, there were only 85 survivors, of whom 80 were members of the crew. Among them was the ship's chief engineer, Eben Abbott, whose immediate responsibility should have been to see that the hoses had ample power to operate. Instead, he was away in the very first boat.

For those experienced officers and seamen who remained, the subsequent hours became an unbelievable nightmare. Panic had spread amongst the passengers who refused, for the most part, to obey orders and

Left: Only six hours out from New York harbour, fire broke out on the popular cruise liner, Morro Castle, carrying 318 passengers and 231 crew. The acting captain and some of the crew members remained in the comparative safety of the bows for many hours.

Below: A view of the Morro Castle's promenade deck indicates the extent and ferocity of the fire which resulted in the death of 90 passengers — many of whom were afraid to take to the boats — and 44 members of the crew.

make for the boats. A crew member said later, 'They wouldn't leave. We pleaded with them. We tried to herd them together. Many tried to fight their way past us and get down the ladder to the lower deck. At last we were forced to leave without them, as sparks and cinders were burning the ropes . . . I told the passengers plainly that they must run the risk of getting singed in going to the boats. They did not seem to understand. We got the boats away in the nick of time, or we should all have been burned.'

But as they rowed away in the near-empty lifeboats they left the confused and panic-stricken passengers to fend for themselves. The scenes were indescribable in their horror. Men, women and children milled about the deck in a bizarre variety of clothing. Some were in pyjamas and nightgowns, others, who a little while before had been enjoying some private party, were in evening attire, the women in elegant gowns and with jewels that sparkled in the glow of the fire. They began to huddle together as the flames drew closer and then, as the pitch between the deck planking began to bubble with the heat, began to perform a grotesque *danse macabre* before finally plunging over the side with cries of utter despair.

Soon the flame-lit, heaving water around the liner seemed filled with passengers, mixed in utter confusion, clinging to wreckage or to the few rafts that had been launched. On one occasion a lifeboat, manned by only eight of the crew, passed through a group of men and women who shouted for help and clutched desperately at the gunwales, but the boat moved relentlessly on to disappear into the darkness. Of the 318 passengers, 90 were to die; of the 231 crew, 44.

George Rogers, the chief radio operator, was seated at his instrument, desperately awaiting the return of his first assistant, George Alagna, whom he had sent to the bridge for permission to start transmitting an SOS. As he sat, a wet towel over his face, he watched as paint began to peel off the walls and as a curtain caught fire and dropped down, setting fire to a settee. Soon he could hardly breathe. Finally, after Alagna had returned with a negative and had been sent back again, he tapped out the CQ (Stand by) then continued his agonizing wait. At last Alagna staggered back into the radio cabin and said, 'Okay chief, start sending.'

This was half-an-hour after the fire had first been reported. Precious time had been lost.

Rogers began to tap out his distress call: SOS. SOS. KGOV. TWENTY MILES SOUTH OF SCOTLAND LIGHT. Halfway through a repeat of this message, an explosion rocked the cabin as the batteries blew out, filling the room with fumes of sulphuric acid. Coughing and spluttering, he managed to turn on his auxiliary generator and then tapped out: SOS TWENTY MILES SOUTH OF SCOTLAND LIGHT. CANNOT WORK MUCH LONGER. FIRE DIRECTLY UNDER RADIO. NEED ASSISTANCE IMMEDIATELY.

Another explosion effectively ended all further transmission but the message had been received by several ships in the vicinity and dawn revealed the great bulk of the *Monarch of Bermuda*, together with the *City of Savannah*, *Andrea F. Luckenbach* and others, all answering the call. The *Monarch of Bermuda* was the nearest vessel and her captain, Albert Francis 'saw a

lot of men on the poop deck of the *Morro Castle* hanging over the side and yelling for assistance.' He and others on his ship also saw an incredible sight. Many of the *Morro Castle*'s passengers, trapped in their cabins, had tried to escape by squeezing through the portholes. These were far too small, however, and most of the desperate people had become helplessly stuck, the expression on their faces revealing the agony of being burnt alive. As a passenger on the *Monarch of Bermuda* said : 'The grimaces made by the people in agony at the portholes was something that I shall never forget. On the deck we saw a young fellow with his wife. She fainted in his arms, and a huge tongue of flame popped out from the wall and sucked them in. We saw a man in pyjamas go up like a torch . . .'

By noon the only signs of life aboard the fiercely burning liner was in her bows where Warms and a few of his men were now stationed. A coastguard cutter, the *Tampa*, nosed as near as it dared and offered to take them off, but Warms refused – his ship was still afloat, he said. This offer was repeated several times but each time Warms replied, 'Not until the *Morro Castle* is in tow.'

The ship was held by an anchor which had been dropped to stop her colliding with rescue ships and this had to be weighed before the ship could be towed away, but there was no power, no winches. Two of Warm's men, however, had small hacksaws in their pockets, and for the next five hours they laboriously sawed through the three-inch anchor-cable, finally freeing the vessel. A hawser was then passed across but snapped as the storm increased.

One by one, the 14 crewmen, including a 14-year-old bell-boy who had elected to stay with them, were finally taken off. At last Warms also agreed to leave his ship and board the *Tampa*, but only after the commander had threatened to use force. Another hawser was passed and the tow began. At first all went well, the cutter towing ahead and a pilot boat acting as a jury rudder astern, but when both ropes parted the liner was abandoned to slowly drift shorewards, still burning furiously, with her paint peeling off in swathes from her once glossy sides, listing at an angle of 30 degrees. Narrowly missing a pier, she came to rest near

the broadwalk at Asbury Park, between New York and Atlantic City, a popular convention and 'fun' town on the Atlantic seaboard.

News of the disaster had already been heard on the radio and by first light a dense crowd of sightseers had assembled to stare seawards as the flame and smoke-blackened liner drifted towards the shore. By noon, owners of ice-cream stalls, hot-dog and frozen-custard stands were eagerly coaxing every cent from this out-of-season show; families stood watching, while bodies were carried up the beach as they were washed ashore. Hawkers also moved amongst the steadily increasing crowds selling pieces of 'genuine' wreckage at a dollar a time.

By early afternoon the crowd had increased to a quarter of a million people and squads of regular soldiers, armed with rifles, were rushed to the scene to drive the mob like sheep before them and establish safety zones around the place where the ship lay beached. Scores of reporters also arrived and the stories they gathered were extremely harrowing.

An inquiry was soon opened before a Federal Grand Jury and proved to be a particularly outspoken one. Warms faced a number of charges, including failure to exercize discipline and control; to arouse the passengers or provide them with lifebelts; to organize the crew to escort the passengers to the boats; to fight the fire; and failure to send out the SOS promptly. He also came in for special criticism when it was disclosed that the liner had been allowed to steam at full speed into a steady head wind which helped fan the flames. Warms, Chief Engineer Abbott and Henry E. Cabaud, executive vice-president of the Ward Line, were arrested, found guilty and sentenced to imprisonment. This sentence, however, was set aside on appeal. The Line itself was fined $10,000 and also had to settle claims amounting to nearly a million dollars.

The inquiry did not establish the cause of the fire. Most experts agreed that a carelessly dropped cigarette had been responsible; others believed that the funnel passing close behind the library walls had overheated them. The loss of life was more simply explained. It was due to naked, uncontrollable panic. On the part of the passengers this was understandable: thrust suddenly into a situation where a horrible death threatened from red fire or black water, their loss of control was excusable.

For Warms, an experienced seaman, there was no such excuse. Faced with sudden responsibility involving his first command and the lives of his passengers and crew, he also cracked, but in a less obvious way. Alagna said at the trial that Warms was 'behaving like a madman'. When the crisis came, he was unable to cope.

That was not the end of the story. The 'hero', Rogers, for a time earned his living recounting the events of that fateful night in vaudeville theatres throughout the U.S.A., but was later convicted of attempted murder and died in gaol. His assistant, Alagna, whose evidence against Warms helped convict that unfortunate officer, later tried to commit suicide.

Not long afterwards the once majestic vessel was towed to Baltimore to be scrapped. She had originally cost five million dollars; she was sold for less than $34,000. Her name passed into history as the principal in one of the ghastliest sea tragedies of all time.

A lucky survivor, Miss Helen Hozanka, is helped down the gangway of a rescue ship on arrival in New York. Several ships were in the vicinity when the fire broke out, and the Monarch of Bermuda *saved many men who were hanging from the poop deck of the* Morro Castle *and yelling for assistance.*

Below: The last hours of the Morro Castle. *Attempts to tow the blazing ship to safety failed, and when the tow ropes parted she was left to drift towards the shore at Asbury Park, New Jersey. There, so many thousands of people came to stare at her that soldiers had to be brought in to clear the crowds.*

HMS Thetis, 1939
and
USS Thresher, 1963

In Birkenhead, Frank Shaw, an engine fitter at Cammell Laird's, lay critically ill. Over and over again he would relive those last hours in H.M.S. *Thetis* in which 99 men died.

Three days previously, on Thursday 1 June 1939, the sleek grey shape of *Thetis* had moved out of Cammell Laird's yard at Birkenhead to undergo simple diving trials. She displaced nearly 1,100 tonnes, one of the latest 'T' class submarines and the first to be built at the Birkenhead yard. Not having been officially handed over to the Admiralty she carried 50 passengers, shipyard men mostly, with a number of extra officers including the senior flotilla officer, Captain H. P. K. Oram. With her five officers and crew of 48 there were 103 men on board and, with the tug *Grebecock* as escort, she left the river and was soon dipping to the surge of the open sea.

At 13.40, some 15 miles west of Great Ormes Head, her captain, Lieutenant-Commander G. H. Bolus, sent a signal to the Flag Officer Submarines (FOSM) at Fort Blockhouse, Gosport, to report that the submarine would be diving for three hours; and almost immediately Lieutenant Coltar, liaison officer on *Grebecock* received the laconic message, 'Diving'. Coltar watched as *Thetis* settled lower in the water, making a perfect dive in 'slow time', then as he was about to turn away he saw her break surface and a sudden splash of air beneath her bows. She then dived horizontally and fairly fast.

Coltar stood watching. The submarine should have dived to periscope depth before descending to 59 feet, firing smoke candles. Nothing happened, so he ordered the tug's captain to stop engines and only use them at intervals to combat a two-knot tide so that she could remain in the vicinity until *Thetis* surfaced once more. Later, Coltar signalled FOSM to ask how long *Thetis* was due to dive. He avoided expressing his personal concern as he did not wish the signal to be picked up by others for, owing to the short range of the tug's radio, the message had to be sent through the Post Office telegraph system. It did not arrive at Gosport until 18.15 due to a series of misfortunes, one of which was the telegraph boy's bicycle having a puncture en route. By then the Duty Officer to FOSM was also worried, having had no direct signal from *Thetis*, and the message from *Grebecock* confirmed his uneasiness.

At 18.50 a call went to the destroyer *Brazen* in the Irish Sea, but as she had only one boiler alight she had to flash up the rest before she could work up to full speed. The Duty Officer at Abbotsfield aerodrome then received a telephone call at 18.50 asking him to organize a search, but as none of the aircraft was in a state of readiness it was nearly an hour before four Ansons

were airborne. By the time they arrived at the disaster area, night had fallen and they had to return. The captain of *Brazen*, seeing the squat outline of the tug against the setting sun was able to ascertain what had happened. Told that *Grebecock* was anchored roughly where *Thetis* had dived, *Brazen* began an ASDIC sweep. In fact, the tug had drifted at least four miles from the actual point of diving and she was making her search *away* from the submarine.

What had caused this urgent, if somewhat delayed, activity?

Bolus had found *Thetis* acting strangely when he first attempted to take her down, and he ordered Lieutenant Frederick Woods to check the forward torpedo tubes. A buoyancy plan showed that tubes 5 and 6, being empty of torpedoes, should be flooded to compensate. Woods checked the valve of No. 5 and no water came out. He was not to know that during construction the outlet hole in the valve had been enamelled over. He decided to open the rear door of the tube to assure himself that there was no water inside. With a rating's help he tugged the door open–and a flood of water cascaded through. By some mischance the tube's bow cap was open to the sea and the tube was completely filled with water. Woods struggled to a telephone and managed to gasp out, 'We're flooding fast through number five tube. Blow main ballast!' then ordered the forward compartment to be evacuated. They then tried to close the watertight door between the forward and the next compartment but one of the bolts had jammed and that also had to be evacuated. Now, with her two forward compartments filling rapidly, *Thetis* dipped and her bows ran into the mud of the sea-bed. Bolus was trying to blow his main ballast and go full astern on his motors but the vessel was too deeply embedded, and remained fast. Finally her stern settled down and the submarine lay in an horizontal position.

The occupants, naval and civilian alike, kept remarkably cool, chatting about sport and joking about a farewell party they would have on their return. There was no panic, but Bolus and Oram, his senior, were concerned about the air supply. The Admiralty had already announced that there was enough for at least 36 hours, quite overlooking the fact that *Thetis* carried double her usual complement which would cut the supply to 18 hours. The two officers then decided to send someone to the surface by means of the after escape chamber to request that a high-pressure hose be connected to the submarine to blow out the flood water.

As there was no indication that rescue craft had arrived overhead, it was probable that anyone being shot to the surface would find himself in an empty sea. Nevertheless, Oram and Woods volunteered to go and after the former had taped messages from the men about his wrist together with details of what had happened should his drowned body be found, both men climbed into their Davis Escape Apparatus and entered the escape chamber. It flooded, they pushed open the escape hatch and within seconds they had shot through 20 feet of sea to arrive, bobbing, on the surface.

Soon after first light *Brazen* had sighted the submarine's stern sticking out of the water and had lowered two whalers to patrol. Oram and Woods were quickly spotted and were soon on board *Brazen* with the first real news of the disaster. Before Oram left the sub-

The tragic Thetis *was salvaged from the seabed on the day that Britain declared war on Germany. She was refitted and, under the name of* Thunderbolt, *went out on her first mission. Before she was finally sunk by an Italian sloop in 1943, she had sunk hundreds of tons of enemy merchant shipping.*

Previous pages: On 3 June 1939 the submarine Thetis *made a trial dive in shallow water off Birkenhead. Despite the fact that, with her bow stuck in the mud, her stern could be clearly seen, rescue work failed and 99 men died.*

marine he had given orders that the remaining men should escape in pairs, a member of the crew and a civilian, but conditions soon deteriorated so much that Bolus, propped against the engine-room door, decided to send four men through the escape chamber at a time. One of the civilians panicked, tore out the mouthpiece of his apparatus and dislodged those of his companions. The chamber was emptied again and when the occupants were dragged out, three were found dead and the survivor managed to gasp that the hatch was jammed before slumping into unconsciousness.

Some indecision followed about who should go next and Frank Shaw found himself pushed forward with Leading Stoker 'Mac' Arnold. Both went into the escape chamber, the rating hurriedly showing Shaw how to fix his apparatus, then signalled for the water to be let in. When, in obedience to the other's signal Shaw helped him push against the hatch, it opened easily. Both men then shot to the surface to be picked up by *Brazen*'s whaler.

Arnold, obviously a man of few words, sent home a telegram reading, 'Am Oke. Mac', while Shaw was taken to his home in Ivydale Road, Birkenhead, and put to bed.

By then a fleet of would-be rescue ships were milling about the spot and divers, oxyacetylene gear and air compressors were demanded; as the stern of the submarine was clearly visible above the surface it was hoped that rescue would soon take place. The first task would be to pump fresh air into her: a diver went down, but he had only half an hour to do the work and was unable to complete the job in time. A wire hawser was placed around *Thetis*'s stern and two tugs took the strain. It was planned to open an aft manhole for fresh air, but at 14.40 *Thetis* suddenly swung around and sank.

Those locked inside the submarine were growing steadily weaker. They had been cheered by the sound of tapping on the hull; at least it seemed a link with the outside world. The divers, too, were gratified when answering taps were received but they grew weaker and then ceased.

Ten minutes after midnight on Saturday, 3 June a hushed crowd clustered about the gates of Cammell Laird's shipyard in Birkenhead to hear a company official say: 'I am sorry but there is no hope for the men remaining in the submarine.' The death-toll was 99 men.

By morning, hundreds of people were thronging the streets demanding a public inquiry, many complaining that the rescue work had been 'bungled'. Others wanted to know why a hole was not cut in the vessel's stern while it was out of the water? Why the stern was not properly secured by hawsers and held above the water as the tide rose? Why *Thetis* had dived in only 130 feet of water? Few of these and other questions were ever satisfactorily answered.

At the inquiry Captain Oram said: 'I would like to make known the excellent behaviour of all the men on board. I saw no sign of panic at any time. I heard men talking and joking until the foul air caused them to keep quiet; and they showed a quiet bravery which is a memory which will live with me for ever.'

* * * *

Postscript. It was decided to salvage *Thetis* as quickly as possible and she was lifted from the seabed on Sunday, 3 September 1939 – the day on which Britain declared war on Germany. She was returned to Cammell Laird's yard and made fighting fit once more. Then, under the name of *Thunderbolt*, she moved out on her first mission which resulted in her torpedoing an Italian submarine. She went on to torpedo another and to sink a considerable amount of enemy merchant shipping until, on 13 March 1943 she was finally sunk by an Italian sloop, *Cigogna*. Her second 'death' was final . . . and honourable.

* * * *

Following the first radio reports that a nuclear submarine was missing, the American nation, and later the world, waited anxiously for more definite news. It came on 11 April 1963 when Admiral George W. Anderson, Chief of Naval Operations, announced grimly: 'Very reluctantly I have come to the conclusion that the *Thresher* has indeed been lost.'

This was the worst submarine disaster in American naval history – 129 deaths including 18 civilians – and the first time that a nuclear submarine had been lost. When launched, *Thresher* was the first of her class, nuclear-powered, 3,750 tons and with a submerged speed of up to 25 knots. She had been launched in July 1960 from the Portsmouth Naval Yard, New Hampshire, representing some $45 million of U.S. taxpayers' money.

Thresher, accompanied by her rescue vessel *Skylark*, began a routine deep dive some 220 miles off Cape Cod in the Gulf of Maine during the morning of Wednesday, 10 April 1963. It was a chill, blustery day with the wind-blown spray showing white around both vessels as the dive began, *Thresher*'s first for some time. Her career had not been a happy one; she had spent nearly half of her two-year life in dock, for repairs and overhauls. She had just slipped from Portsmouth, New Hampshire after a nine-month spell during which she had new equipment installed. That morning was, in effect, part of a shake-down cruise.

At 07.47 *Thresher* signalled that she was preparing to make her deep test dive, and Lieutenant Watson of *Skylark* asked her to give a 'Gertrude check' (navy parlance for underwater telephone communication) every 15 minutes. This was acknowledged, and then her long grey shape slid lower and lower in the water until she had disappeared, contact being maintained by the brief reports at the agreed intervals. At 09.02 she asked for a final confirmation of her course, communication being excellent; then came a call: 'Experiencing minor difficulty. Have positive angle. Am attempting to blow. Will keep you informed.'

To those on board *Skylark* this seemed to imply that the submarine was attempting to close her water vents and to blow air through the manifold system in order to surface, but Watson, listening intently, heard sounds of air under pressure. He summoned his captain, Commander Hecker, to the telephone. Hecker began to call, urgently, 'Are you in control? Are you in control?' but there was no reply. Then, at 19.17 the telephone crackled with a strange garbled message which ended with a word which *could* have been 'exceeding' and then two distinct words . . . 'test depth'.

Then there was silence. It was *Thresher*'s last message.

At 10.58 *Skylark* began dropping hand grenades into the water as a signal to *Thresher* to answer by telephone, but there was no response. The green depths beneath her keel remained as still and silent as the tomb they had so suddenly become.

Rescue ships were rushed to the disaster area and began desperately to search for something – anything – that would give the searchers a lead. The U.S. destroyer *Warrington* reported finding red and yellow gloves and pieces of plastic floating in an oil slick. The gloves were of the kind used by personnel working in the reactor section, the plastic similar to that used to keep the reactor from spreading radiation throughout the craft. The U.S. destroyer *Hazelwood* also came plunging to the scene of the sinking, bringing five civilian scientists and their precision instruments with which, it was hoped, they would be able to locate and fix the position of *Thresher* which by then was resting on the sea bed. But the sea had got up considerably, and winds of 50 m.p.h. screaming from the north-west prevented any accurate or sustained investigation.

It was now debatable whether there was anything to find. *Thresher* had a total depth potential of 1,000 feet, and the ocean bed was more than eight times that depth; no hull yet built could withstand such pressure.

As a submarine descends, its cylindrical-shaped hull, built with heavy steel plates welded to circular 'frames', or ribs, even under normal circumstances becomes compressed by the tremendous weight of the water outside the hull; more than 44 pounds per square inch per 100 feet of depth, and even at 500 feet a submarine creaks and groans as if in protest against such pressure.

Before the inquiry of 4 April 1963, naval technicians and experts alike were endeavouring to determine, on the little evidence to hand, what had actually happened. Some said that the diving planes had jammed during the dive, thrusting her further and further down, a theory dismissed by the more knowledgeable, for had the electro-hydraulic plane control system failed, *Thresher* had two alternative systems that could have been switched on in a matter of seconds. What was more likely was that the pressure had started a major leak, a pipe fitting or intake had failed, or that the pressure hull had suddenly ruptured at a place where a pipe pierced the hull – always a danger point.

Only underwater photographs would reveal the cause of the disaster, and at the depth *Thresher* was lying only one ship in the world was capable of taking them satisfactorily. This was the bathyscaphe, *Trieste II*, an improved version of the original Italian *Trieste* of 1953, which had been bought by the U.S. Office of Naval Research in 1958. At the time of the disaster, *Trieste II* was lying at San Diego on the west coast, and it would be months before the cumbersome craft could be brought to New England. Even so, with closed-circuit television and underwater cameras, and the ability to get close to her subject, she was the obvious – and only – ship which would clearly be suitable for the work ahead.

Until her arrival, a detailed surface and sonar search of the area was carried out and a fleet of vessels, including *Atlantis II*, the world's latest oceanographic ship,

battled 13-feet-high waves and winds. The most sophisticated equipment was used to map the sea-bed at a depth of one and a half miles. The incredibly precise depth-sounders (fathometers) revealed only boulders and rocky ridges, while the surface of the water still ruled out accurate detection by sonar. Nevertheless, something like 100,000 photographs were taken of the calculated area, which was roughly 10 miles square, to make it the most photographed and most charted area in the world.

The inquiry began. The first witness was Commander Dean L. Axene, who had been the commanding officer of *Thresher* from her commissioning in August 1961 until January 1963, when he was relieved by Lt-Commander John W. Harvey, who had gone down with his ship. When asked for his opinion he said he felt sure that the vessel had suffered such sudden flooding that there had been no time for a distress to be transmitted, adding that crew and vessel were of the highest standard.

Lieutenant Watson, when called, referred to hearing 'sounds like a ship breaking up – like a compartment collapsing' soon after the last garbled message had been received. Little else came out of the inquiry, except the reassuring statement that there were no signs of radioactivity at the scene of the disaster, and that *Thresher* had not been armed with Polaris missiles. It was finally agreed that the sinking had probably been caused by some structural or metallurgical defect probably originating in the boat's atomic power plant. For officials of the U.S. naval reactor programme, which until then had achieved a most impressive safety record, this finding was a profound psychological setback.

Outside the court of inquiry, however, other causes were mentioned. Inevitably sabotage was one. People recalled how, at the same naval yard when the original atomic submarine *Nautilus* was being overhauled in 1959, electric cables were found to have been deliberately cut in several places. More dramatic, however, were the comments of some of the unfortunate widows of the crew.

One stated that her husband, on leaving her to join *Thresher* on that last fateful voyage said: 'Honey, I have a feeling that this will be our last trip and that you will be a wealthy widow before the week is out', referring to the generous compensation paid by the U.S. Government under such circumstances. Another woman, widow of one of the submarine's machinist mates recalled bitterly: 'He called it a coffin. He was scared to death to go out in her.'

After a passage of two and a half months, *Trieste II* arrived and began diving operations. She descended to the sea-bed – for her a nominal depth – and eventually squatted alongside the tragic remains of the submarine, photographing the conning-tower, the tail-structure and the débris that had spilled from her interior. The pressure hull was mainly hidden in the sea-bed, having rammed itself into the sand when it had struck. The captain's reports were necessarily of a technical nature, giving no indication of the emotions of the trapped men during those last ghastly seconds, when jets of sea-water were thrusting themselves into the submarine's hull under incredibly high pressure and when the long sleek boat that had been their stable home was dropping down to its inevitable end.

Nearly thirty years after the tragedy of the Thetis, *the American atomic submarine* Thresher *proceeded to make a routine deep test-dive in waters off Cape Cod. Nobody will ever know definitely what went wrong, for the ship continued her death-bringing dive to depths at which the hull could not sustain the pressure, and where it was impossible to reach her. 129 people, including eighteen civilians died in* Thresher.

The Cocoanut Grove, 1942

'Panic' is an ugly word, but the dictionary definition of 'infectious terror' is strictly applicable to events at The Cocoanut Grove, a glittering night-spot in Boston, Massachusetts, on Saturday, 28 November 1942.

From around 7.00 p.m. crowds had been pouring in through the big revolving doors; locals, servicemen with their girl friends, a big party with 'Buck' Jones, the Hollywood Singing Cowboy, and a large posse of fans celebrating the unexpected victory that day of the Holy Cross football team over Boston College.

Over a thousand people jostled to get into a club licensed for 460, but the club's owner Barney Welansky, gangster and racketeer, had never bothered too much about licences, bye-laws and the rest. The club's two main floors had just been rearranged by him to hold more people. The upstairs restaurant, with revolving stage for floor shows, was slightly below the performers' changing-rooms. On the ground floor was 'The Melody Lounge'.

The 40-foot-square, eating, drinking and dancing Lounge was gaudily exotic. Walls and wall-seats were covered with rexine imitation leather. The low ceiling was draped with coloured silks ballooning down like sunset clouds, and palm trees of *papier mâchè* were dotted among the tables with lacquered paper foliage stretching up to form a leafy trellis. The big curving bar was made of plywood with walnut veneer and the ceiling lights nestled in cocoanut husks. A Hawaiian dream world!

About 10.00 p.m., in an atmosphere more like Hades than Hawaii, one of the guests took out a ceiling bulb near his table. Minutes later, the manager spotted the dim corner and sent a new bulb with a young waiter, Steve Tomaszewski. He couldn't find the socket and lit a match.

Later, after 492 people had died, Steve swore he had flicked out the match. Some accounts tell of a sudden spurt of flame from a nearby palm tree, so perhaps there had been a short-circuit. No one will ever know the exact cause, only the result was clear.

The place was like a tinder-box and within seconds flames were leaping everywhere. The lacquer, paper and silk flared up, and the Lounge was filled with black, asphyxiating smoke.

One of those present, journalist Martin Sheridan, wrote afterwards: 'We had just been served with an oyster cocktail when, above the babble, I thought I heard cries of "Fight". . . Liquor had been flowing freely for hours . . . I thought to myself it must be just a minor brawl. . . . Suddenly someone at the end of our table screamed "FIRE"! Then I heard the loud crackling of flames. . . . A cloud of black smoke surged across the room. . . . No need to get excited, I thought. Just get up casually and walk to the nearest exit.'

The calm ones fared no better than the rest. Sheridan had not taken three steps before he was on the floor, choking and fainting from fumes, the last sounds in his ears the crash of shattered crockery and the screams of terrified people.

Sheridan survived by a fluke. Everyone believed the nearest exit meant the revolving doors, but the big building had no less than nine exits. As well as the main one there were four smaller doors on the east wall including one gained by some stairs and through an office. To the north were four more and on the west side was a single door with a quick-acting release, though this was temporarily jammed. But no one knew about these other exits: they were neither indicated nor illuminated nor even visible by the time Welansky had finished constructing his Hawaiian scene. All but the front windows were boarded up and all had stout metal frames allowing passage for only the smallest bodies.

People surged straight for the revolving doors. Soon the lights failed and many got out only by the glare of flames. One was Joyce Spector who said later: 'I crawled for what seemed to be miles. Suddenly – I don't know how – I was in the street and could feel the cold night air on my face. Then a heavy weight fell on me'. The weight was the body of a man who had stumbled out after her and dropped dead just as he reached safety.

As the smoke and heat intensified, the rush turned to a stampede and the door became blocked. Some people were trampled underfoot. Others were thrusting to get out of the Lounge when suddenly part of the floor gave way and they were hurled to death in the basement. A naval officer later found dead had his jacket clawed from his back. Firemen who soon arrived saw a wall of contorted faces beyond the door and after breaking it down found corpses, grotesquely splayed and entangled six deep.

Some found different escape routes, like Mr John Gill, from Arlington, who dragged his wife towards the sound of breaking glass at the back of the building. 'One moment I was moving towards that sound. . . . The next few seconds or minutes, I couldn't say which, are blanks in my memory. I don't remember that we were borne through that little door, but we must have been. I don't know whether we were shoved or whether we crawled.'

Others escaped through a basement window, a few through other doors, a few more by shutting themselves in a basement refrigeration room until it was safe to come out. Some floor-show performers climbed on to the flat roof, then down to safety by a ladder. A handful were found later, half-dead, halfway to freedom, their bodies wedged in the broken glass of windows.

Four hundred and thirty-three people, including the Singing Cowboy, died inside The Cocoanut Grove, from asphyxiation, suffocation, burns, heart-failure or fractured skulls. A further 59 died in hospital.

Above: Although there were no less than nine exits from The Cocoanut Grove night-spot in Boston, they were neither indicated nor even visible behind the elaborate décor. People struggled to get through the revolving doors of the main entrance.

Labels on image: PARKING SPACE · MAIN ENTRANCE · WHERE ROOF FELL IN · USED FOR MORGUE · PIEDMONT ST. · CHURCH ST.

goat, to some extent, for the omissions of the city's administrators: none of the provisions omitted by Welansky was obligatory by law. Boston's building regulations were inadequate and those that did exist could be evaded, if necessary, by political influence.

The summing up by a County Grand Jury was extraordinarily bland. There had been, it was said, a 'shifting of responsibility and a tendency by various officials in different important departments to rely too much on their subordinates without exercising sufficient and proper check'. The Mayor declared that he had repeatedly reminded the citizens that there was a war on, emergencies might be expected and it was their duty at all times to remain 'calm and quiet, cool and collected'.

In America, the Underwriters' Laboratories began an intensive investigation into the problems of highly combustible interior furnishings and finishes. They issued a report in 1962 and research continues.

In Boston the site of the club has long since become a car-park and there is no Cocoanut Grove in the city, possibly in the whole of America. In Britain, the lessons to be drawn from the calamity still feature in fire-prevention courses.

Below: Over a thousand people poured into a building licensed for 460. Such was the panic that broke out in the overcrowded rooms that 433 people died from asphyxiation, suffocation, burns, heart failure and fractured skulls. And although rescue workers were quickly on the spot another 59 people died later in hospital.

The fire was put out within an hour, but rescue work went on all night, helped by the Civil Defence and the Red Cross. Anti-burn drugs were rushed from New York. Local hospitals, where one casualty was being admitted every ten seconds and the corridors were lined with dead bodies awaiting identification, had to open their wartime blood plasma banks. Passing vehicles of every kind were flagged down to provide transport. All night, crowds of sightseers converged on the scene, impeding the work, until martial law was declared in the early hours.

Next day there was a hurried examination of other Boston night-clubs for similar hazards. Then a grand inquiry was held into causes and responsibilities. The immediate cause of the fire was never established. But once started, why did it end in disaster? The answers were clear, and bad for Welansky. No planning permission had been obtained for his 'Melody Lounge', nor permits granted for electrical work carried out by unqualified men. The exits were neither illuminated nor indicated. The club had no emergency lighting or automatic fire-sprinklers and – important for slowly recovering survivors – was not covered by insurance for guests.

Welansky got 12 years in jail, but was released, after three, in 1946, with incurable cancer. He was the scape-

Naples Black Market Express, 1944

Incredibly, a whole train load of 521 people died in one of the eeriest train disasters of all time. Brought to a halt by icy, slippery rails in a narrow two-mile long tunnel, it is assumed that carbon monoxide gas produced by the vainly labouring engine overcame the passengers as they sat in their seats. Only the brakeman and five passengers survived.

World War II provided the most bizarre railway catastrophe of all time. Train No. 8017, which ran between Naples and Lucania every Thursday night, was known as the Black Market Express. It carried 520 passengers, most of them the professional black marketeers of Naples who made this regular journey to fill their bags with meats, grains, vegetables, oils, tobacco and sweets for Naples, then (in March 1944) occupied by the Allied Forces.

Although *la borsa nera* (the black market) was prohibited, the Allied Military Government and the Italian officials realized that if these black marketeers did not use Train 8017 to bring in illegal supplies, there would be hardly enough food available for the million inhabitants of Naples.

On the night of 2 March 1944, the train pulled out of Naples with 521 passengers and six railway workers: the 8017 had 42 box-cars (empty), two steam-engines, four coaches and one caboose. On all its previous trips two engines had been used, as the total weight of the train had never exceeded 500 tons but, on this fateful journey, medical students from Bari were returning from a hospital field exercise. Total weight touched 511 tons – 11 tons over the maximum for a two-engine pull.

The 8017 might have got away with the overloading, but some parts of the Naples-Lucania line had stretches of ice-coated upgrade rails. If it had not attempted to hit top speed on these stretches the chances were that the slippery tracks would prove impassable.

After it pulled out of Balvano-Ricigliano station on the Apennine Mountain chain, the station-master said goodnight to his staff and left some instructions with his assistant, Giuseppe Salonia, for his spell of duty. These done, Salonia curled up with his newspaper for

the next hour or so. Just before the next train was scheduled to enter Balvano, he remembered that he had not received any ticker-tape message about the 8017's arrival at Bella-Muro, its next stop nearly four miles further on, thus telling Salonia that the single track would be all clear for use.

Instead, Salonia was told by the Bella-Muro station that the 8017 was running nearly two hours late. He replied that he would hold the 8025 at Balvano and would check the single track himself with a free locomotive. At 2.40 a.m. the 8025 rumbled into the station. Salonia ordered two trackmen, Caponegro and Biondi, to detach the engine from the train so that he could inspect the track leading to Bella-Muro.

The big mystery was the fate of the 8017 from the time it left Balvano station. Moments before it drew out, the train's chief engineer, Gigliani, in the leading engine had ordered his fireman, Rosario Barbato, to shovel a particularly large dosage of coal into the engine's furnace–'We'll need it for these upgradients later', he had said.

The train had no trouble making the incline within the first tunnel, and puffed through the second reasonably well. Then it emerged on to a snaky viaduct about 25 yards long which fed into a forest-girt S-curve tunnel, the Galleria delle Armi, two miles long. At this disaster-point no-one can be 100 per cent sure what happened. It has been reasoned that the man at the throttle was worried by the high reading on his furnace-pressure gauge which apparently did not correspond with the engine speed, and the train must have been slowing badly in the damp narrow tunnel with its steep incline.

When all the cars, except the caboose, had entered the underground passageway, the 8017 groaned to a standstill under the excess weight on icy rails. Meanwhile, in the caboose brakeman Michele Palo was trying to keep himself warm; the engineer had not pulled the whistle-cord to give warning that anything was amiss so Palo assumed that the train had stopped for a signal of some kind – by no means an unusual event on a railway . . .

Finally he decided to take some action. He forced open a lower window and stuck his head out, but the whole train seemed to be encased in the black hole that bored through the hillside. The brakeman drew on his gloves and swung down from his caboose to find out what was holding things up. He had gone no further than a few yards into the black hole when he realized what had happened.

At once he turned round and ran along the track towards the Balvano depot two miles away downhill. He hoped to arrive in about an hour and get help for some of those aboard 8017. But his nightmare jog-trot took him much, much longer than that – most of the time he found himself forced down on hands and knees.

It was 2.50 a.m. when he came within sight of Balvano
– at about the same time as Salonia had boarded the
engine and started it up. Palo swung his red lantern
from the mouth of the Balvano tunnel and yelled: 'Up
the track!' 'Up the track!' When Salonia reached Palo
he had collapsed on the line, and was moaning '*Sono
tutti morti!*' ('They're all dead!')

Salonia had heard no crash, saw no evidence of an
accident. Could the 8017 have left the rails? Not
possible, Salonia decided, or some noise would have
been heard in that snow-hushed countryside. He concluded that Palo had taken leave of his senses – the man
was sobbing bitterly and every now and then buried his
face in the station-master's jacket. Salonia picked the
distraught railwayman up in his arms and carried him
to the station where he was gently coaxed to relate what
he could remember.

It was now almost 4.00 a.m. Despite the hour, everyone of importance in the town of Balvano was aroused.
Salonia edged the 8025 engine slowly up the track to
the tunnel Galleria delle Armi. He stopped the 8025
and, in the early morning mist, he made his way on foot
to the last car of the 8017 which was held in the tunnel.

There was no sign of an accident, only an eerie, un-
natural silence. Salonia slid open the door of one car
and entered, lighting the interior with his lantern. Passengers were seated and sprawled in postures of utter
relaxation. They looked as if they were asleep, but they
were all dead. In every car Salonia entered, the scene
was repeated: not one of the 500 showed the slightest
flicker of life. The men in the cab were dead too, the
engineer still at his throttle with his head rested on the
side of the window-pane.

Salonia broke down, hardly able to bear the evidence
of his eyes. He took a grip on himself, undid the brakes
and backed the 8017 to the engine of his 8025, hitched
the engine to the 8017 caboose, and towed the train of
peaceful death back to Balvano. The police took over
the macabre duty of carrying out the dead and laying
them side by side on the station platform for future
identification.

In all, 521 people died in the eeriest railway disaster
of the century. The Italian State police had the task of
reconstructing what must have happened inside the
mountain. The 8017 could not have gone very far into
the tunnel before its wheels began to slide. Chief
engineer Gigliani could easily have backed the train
downhill out of the tunnel and on to the viaduct. Instead
he chose to press on in a bid to get over the gradient that
impeded the train's forward impetus. The four crewmen in the two locomotive compartments – Gigliani
and stoker Barbato in the leading engine, throttler
Senatore and foreman Ronga in the second cab – set
about scooping coal into the firebox. They worked like
men possessed, yet the huge wheels, having lost all grip
on the rails, simply spun faster and faster over the
slippery track, and the train stayed on the same spot.

As the roaring fires devoured the emergency supply
of soft coal, not one of the sweating crewmen realized
that the fuel was producing lethal carbon-monoxide
gas. The passengers – most of whom were asleep – did
not worry because the train had stopped within a mountain. The carbon-monoxide took the lives of the four
men in the engines, then worked its deadly way through
the lungs of the conductor and 516 passengers.

BALVANO.RICIGLIANO

Police, checking every detail, found that five passengers had not been suffocated by the gas; three were
black marketeers who were brought to the station-
master's office for medical treatment. Later they disappeared discreetly to avoid the questioning which
would certainly have exposed their illegal activities, so
they were of no help to the police in tackling the
mysteries surrounding the 8017.

One survivor, an olive-oil salesman named Domenico
Miele, was to prove of great value. He reported that he
had stepped off the train at Balvano to stretch his legs
for a few minutes. Finding the cold air too much for
him, he took a scarf from his luggage, an action which
was to save his life. When the train came to a dead
stop inside the tunnel, Miele was one of the few who
had not dropped off to sleep.

When the carbon-monoxide gas reached him, it
started him coughing. Miele wrapped his scarf round
his mouth as a filter, got off the train and made an un-
steady way out of the tunnel. He did not guess that there
was killer gas about because he climbed into the next,
and last, coach to find another seat, but only reached
the vestibule where he fainted and remained prostrate
until he was picked up by two policemen who presumed
him dead and carried him off to the improvised
mortuary on the Balvano station platform.

As a result of partial gas poisoning Miele's hair (so
says the official police report on the tragedy) turned
from a rich black colour to a soapy grey.

The other surviving passenger was found, a small
dealer named Luigi Cozzolino, but he suffered such
severe brain damage that he did not realize what had
happened, not even that his wife and eight-year-old son
died on that ill-fated 8017.

Because of wartime censorship only one newspaper
was allowed to publish a short official notice about the
'mishap'. All lawsuits were ruled out of order because
the Allied Military Government had been technically
in charge of Italy's railway system and could not be held
accountable in law for a 'wartime accident'.

*Rescue services from
the neighbouring town
of Balvano could do
nothing. Their only
function was to lay
out the bodies along
the railway lines and
later drive them in
lorry loads to the
mortuary.*

Burnden Park, 1946 and Ibrox Park, 1971

The football fans of Britain, starved of their favourite sport during World War II, were packing the grounds during the first full soccer season since the war's end – and 70,000 of them headed for Burnden Park, Bolton, in Lancashire on 9 March 1946, to watch the local Wanderers at the peak of their success.

Bolton Wanderers had enjoyed a long and glorious history, having won the Football Association Cup outright three times and reached the last four semi-finals nine times. Now they were poised to reach their tenth F.A. Cup semi-final, and they had already defeated their opponents, Stoke City, 2–0 away from home in the first leg of this cup-tie.

Although it was obvious that the Bolton ground would be packed to capacity that afternoon, the Darcy Lever stand, which could seat 2,800 people, stood conspicuously empty; the surrounding terraces were all jammed with a dangerous mass of swaying and singing supporters. Why this apparently ridiculous contradiction? The stand had been used during the war as a storage shed for the Ministry of Supply, and it seems that the Bolton police had refused the club permission to use it during the match because of fire hazards . . .

That there was a deadlier hazard – overcrowding – was to become apparent all too soon. Behind one side of the ground the railway ran over an embankment, and in front of that embankment was the enclosed space of the ground's 'railway end'. It was here that the press of teeming banks of supporters was at its worst. The entire length of the road leading to the turnstiles at this end was a solid mass and, with each passing minute, it grew in depth as more and more fans joined it, inexorably increasing the pressure.

One newspaper-man who turned up there just after 2 p.m. – kick-off was due an hour later – reported that he found himself so hemmed in that he could not move forward or backward. 'Before I had a chance to get away', he wrote, 'I was gripped so tightly that I swayed and struggled, sweated and swore for the next hour in a cursing, roaring, mauling crowd of about 15,000 people in that enclosure alone.'

At 2.40 p.m. police ordered the turnstiles at the embankment end to be locked – Burnden Park was now bulging at the seams; every vantage point offering a view of the playing field was occupied and anything that could be climbed inside the ground had been scaled. Spectators were perched precariously on the roofs of refreshment huts and balanced uncomfortably on boundary fences. Men scrambled up the walls of the stands, skidded across sloping roofs, hauled themselves somehow on to huge advertisement hoardings in a desperate attempt to get a bird's-eye view of the game.

The police had to close the turnstiles, but the effect of this decision was to bottle up the embankment end of the ground. As a result this densely packed wedge of humanity became a potential battering-ram. It took some time to realize that a situation of crisis proportions had built up. Then the aged and the children began to collapse and were passed over the sea of bobbing heads to comparative safety.

Suddenly a great and growing roar swelled inside the ground . . . the teams were in position and the game was about to begin: the long build-up of excitement had reached climax-point. When the referee blew his whistle for the kick-off most spectators became so absorbed in the game that they were oblivious of the life-and-death struggle now raging in earnest at the embankment end of the ground. Of the thousands locked out by the police order to close the turnstiles, hundreds now began to force a way past the thin blue line of policemen guarding the railway embankment itself. They smashed their passage through sleeper fencing and some found a grandstand seat on a well-placed shunting engine and its goods wagons in the siding.

But others insisted on hacking and barging their way into the already teeming enclosure, swelling the crowd there to beyond bursting point. Something had to give, the cauldron had to blow its top . . . A running-track circled the ground between the pitch and the terraces and on this track stood a ring of police; their normal duty was to prevent enthusiasts rushing on to the playing area. But this police guard was the first to appreciate that the crowds swaying and yelling on the embankment were convulsed not by football excitement but by stark fear.

Policemen rushed to rip away part of the fencing holding back these spectators from the safety of the running-track, but their action came too late. A low wall on the terracing gave way, two steel crush barriers collapsed and an uncontrollable tidal wave of humanity surged forward and down. Men, women and children were stacked up in piles like broken dolls. Those who could, scrambled over the rails on to the track, and hundreds of others swept to the edge of the playing pitch; all this time the players, the referee and, indeed,

the vast majority of the 70,000 crowd inside the ground were utterly unaware of the disaster in their midst.

At last a police inspector ran across the pitch to implore the referee to stop the game – he did so at once and led the players from the field. Still most of the spectators were ignorant of the tragedy – to them the prostrate bodies looked like fainting cases, a common enough sight at soccer games.

The officials on duty realized only too well that they had a major disaster to deal with. An SOS went out for doctors, ambulances and oxygen cylinders. Gradually the extent of the tragedy began to dawn on the thousands who still milled around in the adjoining streets outside Burnden Park, when they saw the stream of ambulances arrive and the seemingly endless procession of stretchers carrying dead and seriously injured out of the ground.

Behind the scenes police chiefs conferred with the referee, the officials and the captains of both clubs. The police feared further trouble if the game were abandoned and asked that it be re-started. Already sections of the crowd were giving voice to their impatience. The players eventually returned to the field and played out a goalless draw.

Thus Bolton Wanderers reached their tenth F.A. Cup semi-final. The cost in terms of the accompanying

Football frenzy at its peak caused hundreds of people to force their way into an already overcrowded enclosure. The crowds swaying and yelling on the embankment soon became prey to fear as they realized that disaster threatened. Police rushed, too late, to allow people on to the pitch; the sheer weight of a mass of humanity surged forward in an uncontrollable tidal wave in which men, women and children collapsed in piles, like broken dolls.

Left: Reminiscent of a battlefield is the Ibrox football ground where 66 people died when a crush-barrier collapsed. Bodies of some of the victims are laid out on the goal line while doctors, nurses, police and other rescue workers tend some of the hundred people who were injured.

Previous pages: Some of the injured brought out from among the vast crowd which attended a cup final match at Burnden Park, Bolton, Lancashire. Part of the crowd surged forward, trampling those in front of them, and killing 33 people.

human tragedy was 33 killed and 500 injured. It was, until dwarfed by the appalling disaster at Ibrox Park, the worst football tragedy Britain had ever experienced.

*　　*　　*　　*

The worst spectator disaster in the long history of British football killed 66 people and injured 100 in a fearsome stampede down one of the steep stairways leading from the terraces of Ibrox Park, football ground of Glasgow Rangers. It followed the last seconds of the 1971 New Year match between Rangers and Glasgow Celtic, the deadliest rivals in Scottish football. Rangers equalized in the last minute of the game – and police blame that goal for the buckling of a steel barrier under unsupportable pressure.

Thousands of fans were already leaving the ground when a mighty roar stopped them in their tracks. The word flashed round that Rangers had equalized, making the score one all. Many – too many – of the thousands who were leaving the ground tried to turn back, and on the stairway leading to Terrace No. 13 they met a solid mass of spectators coming down. The ensuing build-up of pressure burst the railings of the stairway: some people, children among them, were crushed to death against the iron stanchions; others were suffocated by the weight of bodies falling on top of them.

Fifty-three died inside the stadium and 13 on the way to hospital. Every ambulance in the city of Glasgow was called to Ibrox Park, and police were rushed to the spot – even the mounted police got an SOS; firemen were sent to the ground to light up the huge and now bare stadium.

For many of the 80,000 crowd on 2 January the first hint that something was amiss came when they were walking towards the city centre after the match. Police cars and ambulances by the score flashing blue roof-lights and sounding sirens raced into the streets lined with red-sandstone tenements which border the terracing in Ibrox Park.

Above : The fatal stair-case on which part of the Ibrox crowd attempted to turn as the match ended. They met crowds coming down and the build-up of pressure burst the railings.

Below : A nurse rushes to help the injured.

Inside the high red walls of the ground was a spectacle to turn the strongest stomach . . . corpses lay sprawled at the foot of the stairway which had become a death-trap, and were left unattended while police and firemen tried to revive any who might have a faint chance of life, however slender. Dazed, people were staggering around trying to trace fathers, brothers or friends who had failed to return from the match. They were staring pathetically at the rows of corpses barely concealed under grey sheets on the grassy bank that slopes down behind the wide curve of terraces.

Sir Donald Liddle, the Lord Provost of Glasgow, did his best to hold a Press conference, but broke down at the start and wept. 'The tragedy is enormous', he said in broken tones. 'Words fail me. From seeing the people involved it is obvious that a wide cross-section of the population and all age-groups are affected.'

When the bundles of bodies were disentangled into recognizable human beings it was seen that there were several boys and at least one girl among them. Some were carried down to the pitch and the running-track surrounding it; many were laid out in the gymnasium and offices under the stand.

One witness, shattered by what he saw, said: 'The bodies just kept pouring on top of one another like water over a waterfall.' A policeman remarked: 'I was leaving the match when I heard screaming. I looked back and saw a pile of bodies about 10 feet high all laid the same way with their faces towards me – a wall of faces, some with their tongues lolling out.

'I carried away one little ginger-haired laddie and a colleague tried to give him the kiss of life until a doctor said, "You're wasting your time – the wee boy's dead."

'The injuries of some of those who had been crushed right under the barrier were horrible to see. We came away with our boots, socks and the bottoms of our trousers soaked in blood.'

Tangiwai, 1953

Christmas had a special flavour of delight for the people of New Zealand in 1953. The newly crowned Queen Elizabeth was in their country on a royal visit, and she was to make the traditional Christmas Day broadcast to the Commonwealth from Auckland. Thousands of families travelled from their homes to the places on the Queen's route to catch a glimpse of her. New Zealand was a land of smiles.

One hundred and fifty miles to the south of Auckland, half-way to the city of Wellington, the glowering volcano Ruapehu mumbled and shifted that Christmas Eve. The 9,000-foot mountain is the highest on North Island, and had last stirred eight years earlier. Now it burst into violent wakefulness, erupting in scalding water, mud and rock.

As the volcanic crater split open, the 14-acre lake within it poured down the mountainside and burst out through a cave beneath the Whangaehu Glacier. A large part of the glacier broke up with a roar that was heard at the Waiouru military camp 10 miles away, where soldiers and nurses at the military hospital were enjoying themselves at the Christmas Eve party.

The cascade foaming down the sides of Mount Ruapehu had become what volcanologists call a *lahar*, a type of mud-flow which, as it gains momentum, gathers to itself large quantities of volcanic ash, trees, soil and other débris which together with the water and ice forms a thick slurry. Because of its density this can carry enormous boulders across miles of fairly flat country once the initial momentum has been gained.

The awesome force of this *lahar* burst into the Whangaehu River and joined the current hurtling down the valley carrying great rocks and jagged lumps of ice towards the railway bridge at Tangiwai (a Maori name meaning 'Weeping Waters').

The Tangiwai bridge had been built in 1906 and the rails stood 35 feet over the bed of the river. It was a sturdy construction, 198 feet long, made of steel on concrete piers, but in the path of Nature's unleashed fury it might have been a child's plastic toy. As the *lahar* struck, one of the piers crumpled and joined the onward rush. It was a mortal blow to the bridge.

Cyril Ellis, the local postmaster, heard the roar of the river and went out to investigate. The height of the water was 20 feet above normal, and the railway lines were under its surface. It was 10.21 p.m. and Ellis knew that the main trunk express from Wellington to Auckland was shortly due to pass over the bridge at full speed. He had a powerful electric flash-lamp with him, and he started off down the line in the direction the train would come to stop the Auckland Express from what seemed like certain disaster.

Ellis was already too late. In the distance he saw the light on the powerful locomotive approaching at a good 50 m.p.h. He swung his torch to and fro in the path of the engine, then jumped aside as it passed. He had a

glimpse of the men on the footplate, and screamed at the top of his voice: 'Stop! The bridge has gone!' The driver slammed on the brakes.

With barely 100 yards to the bridge the train squealed along the tracks on locked wheels on to the centre span. The bridge, undermined through the loss of the pier, collapsed in the middle and the 130-ton locomotive dived into the raging torrent and exploded, dragging the first five carriages with it. Ellis watched the lighted carriages slither past him into the river, and heard the screams of the passengers quickly silenced as the water drowned them.

The sixth carriage teetered on the broken edge of the bridge at a 45-degree angle, those behind remaining comparatively steady on the bank. Ellis ran with the guard to the coach on the brink and climbed aboard: 'Everybody out, quick!' he shouted, 'This carriage is going down into the river!'

A moment later the coupling holding it to the seventh carriage snapped and down they went into the water. Three times it rolled over like a log before beaching on the river bank. The carriage was quickly filled with a surge of water, oil and silt, and the passengers were whirled about like corks. Ellis took firm hold of the luggage-rack and managed to keep his head above water. Amazingly his torch still kept alight. He kicked out one of the windows and hoisted himself outside once more. Bracing himself against the coachwork, he hauled people out of the interior. Two other men, John Holman and a man named Hartwell, joined Ellis, and together they crawled along the outside of the carriage, breaking open windows and dragging out the coughing, survivors. Ellis rescued 26 people that night.

To add to the general distress the engine had been towing an oil-tender which had discharged its load into the river, and now everyone was covered with oil as well as silt. The force of the current was so great that the water-sodden clothes were wrenched from their bodies, leaving many of the people naked.

The Christmas Eve express from Wellington to Auckland was carrying a full complement of passengers, on their way to friends and relations for the Christmas holiday, when it roared on to the bridge across the Whangaehu river at Tangiwai. A local resident had tried to stop it, for he knew that a volcanic eruption had brought down a wave of water, mud and rock which had damaged the bridge. He was too late: the 130-ton locomotive, brakes locked, screamed on to the bridge and dived into the raging torrent. Daylight revealed to appalled onlookers the full extent of the disaster.

In mid-stream the depth and speed of the current was carrying everything before it. The five carriages had all their woodwork beaten away and carried downstream, leaving only the mangled iron frames in the vicinity. One carriage and the concrete pier of the bridge were washed along for miles before beaching on an island.

At the road bridge parallel with the rail viaduct, two motorists had drawn up minutes before the catastrophe. Mr Dewar Bell had been driving towards Waiouru with his wife when they came upon the flooded bridge. As Bell stepped out of his car, gazing at the scene with amazement, the ground shook under his feet with the impact of the boulders striking banks and river-bed and the air was vibrating.

Nearby, another motorist had stopped when the caravan he was trailing ran off the road. Together they looked towards the Tangiwai bridge. It was under water. On the far side of the structure the lights of the Auckland Express could be seen, bearing down on the bridge. 'What's going to happen if the bridge isn't there?' yelled Bell to the other motorist. Moments later the doomed train plunged into the river.

While Mrs Bell drove for help, her husband scrambled down to the water's edge. In no more than two feet of water he could barely stand against the force of the current, but he managed to drag several oil-blackened people to the bank. The caravan was used as a makeshift first-aid post. Bell climbed into the carriage lying on the embankment; 20 people, most of them injured, were struggling in three feet of water. Bell began pushing and hauling them out; 16 people owed their salvation to him.

Mrs Bell had found a phone and raised the alarm. At the Waiouru military camp the Christmas dance ended abruptly and nurses piled into lorries with the troops. From the surrounding countryside farmers and clerks and businessmen left their homes to join the volunteers at the scene of suffering.

Along the river bank were many signs that the victims were mostly Christmas holiday-makers returning home with presents; muddy toys, a little girl's doll, a cuddly felt animal, were scattered among the débris.

On the polished dance-floor at Waiouru there soon lay orderly rows of coffins and sheeted corpses. Many had been stripped by the savage water and identification was difficult if not impossible in a number of cases. As a makeshift measure a serial number was chalked on the floor at the feet of each casualty. There were very few injuries for the doctors and nurses to deal with. One of the tragic aspects of Tangiwai was that those who had been injured in the crash almost certainly died in the water, unable to help themselves in the grip of the torrent. For the most part the medical staff had to deal with cases of severe shock.

New Zealand's Prime Minister, Sidney Holland, went immediately to the crash scene. On Christmas Day he spoke to the nation on radio, and read out some of the names of known survivors. The Queen did not go to Tangiwai, having been advised to carry on with her planned programme to avoid disappointing those who were to meet her. At the conclusion of her Christmas Day broadcast she made a moving reference to New Zealand's great sadness.

The Tangiwai tragedy was New Zealand's greatest rail disaster. There had been 285 people on the Auckland Express, of whom 134 were saved. Identified bodies amounted to 123, with a further eight who could not be named; and 20 bodies were not recovered. The unidentified bodies were taken to Wellington for a mass funeral attended by the Duke of Edinburgh.

Before she left New Zealand, the Queen honoured four of the heroes of Tangiwai. Cyril Ellis and John Holman were awarded the George Medal, and Dewar Bell and W. I. Inglis received the British Empire Medal (Civil Division).

The subsequent inquiry concluded that the disaster had been due entirely to capricious Nature.

Such was the depth and speed of the current that the woodwork of five carriages was beaten away. One carriage and the concrete pier of the bridge were carried along for miles before beaching on an island.

Salvage workers in action. Victims and wreckage alike were covered in mud, weeds and oil from the oil tender which the engine had been towing. In all, 135 of the 285 people who had been on the express died.

Le Mans, 1955

Le Mans as we know it is the scene of the world-famous classic motor racing event, the French Grand Prix d'Endurance, a 24-hour non-stop event which has converted this ancient town into a gallic Brands Hatch.

The town-hall is built on the site of a former castle, and the town itself, which lies about 100 miles south-west of Paris, is the seat of a bishopric dating back to the third century A.D. King Henry II of England was born here, and its cathedral houses the tomb of Berengaria of Navarre, wife of England's Richard Coeur de Lion.

Today, Le Mans is synonymous with the best in motor-racing, and it has its own history, of which the most dramatic episode occurred in just a few seconds on Saturday, 11 June 1955. In that instant a Mercedes car, momentarily out of control, rocketed off the track into a part of the crowd of more than a quarter of a million spectators, cut a swathe through them, bounced and then exploded in an incandescent star-burst. In less time than it takes to relate, it killed 82 people and seriously injured more than 100 others.

Shock, frenzy, horror? Certainly, and in full numbing measure – but the officials, with a curious *sang froid*, insisted that the race should continue, complete with its attendant fairground carnival music and amusements, while the police, doctors and ambulancemen gathered the seriously injured, the dead and fragments of the dead, and took them away with speedy efficiency to nearby hospitals and mortuaries.

This particular Le Mans Grand Prix had aroused an enormous amount of international interest. World champion Fangio was competing, and new cars with famous drivers were expected to establish new speed records at, as one newspaper reported, 'a pace never seen here before'. Entrants included Mercedes-Benz of West Germany, the Italian Ferraris and Maseratis, the Gordinis of France, British Jaguars, Aston Martins and so on. It was the days when Fangio, Castelotti and the late Mike Hawthorn were virtually household names, even among the non-aficianados of the sport.

The weather was sunny and hot, and even though some rain was forecast a carnival atmosphere abounded. It was a kind of Royal Ascot of the internal-combustion engine. In the surrounding fairground and bars business boomed as the race got under way in the late afternoon. Bunched together, the leading cars took the bends at 150 m.p.h., and then Fangio and Hawthorn began to break lap records, building up to an average lap speed of 120 m.p.h. – as fast as the fastest of any previous Grand Prix. It was exciting and spellbinding for the first two hours, at which point horror struck like a thunderbolt. One of the Mercedes cars slewed from the track, bounced over the earth safety-bank, rocketed through the massed spectators and finally exploded at a cost of nearly 100 lives, and many injured. Time taken – a matter of two or three seconds.

Precisely how this came about has since been a subject of unending controversy. At the time the contest was running well. The attention of the crowd was centred on Mike Hawthorn in a new D-type Jaguar who was seriously challenging world champion Fangio in his silver Mercedes-Benz. Both had gained a lap on Pierre Levegh, the Frenchman in the Mercedes No. 3 team car. No hazard was evident – the cars were 'all systems go' and the drivers in good trim.

Then Mike Hawthorn began to brake and slow down to pull into his pit on the right so that his co-driver, Londoner Ivor Bueb, could take over. During the subsequent inquiry, and some years later in a letter to *The Times*, Hawthorn was quoted as insisting that he had given the prescribed hand signal in accordance with accepted racing practice. As he slowed and pulled over towards his pit, Levegh's Mercedes came up from behind to pass at around 180 m.p.h. In the resulting swerve the Mercedes touched the rear of a British Austin-Healey driven by Lance Macklin.

All motion is relative. That 'touch' at 180 m.p.h. hurled the Austin-Healey into a frantic broadside skid 100 yards long, but it ended safely enough and few paid much attention. All eyes were on Levegh's Mercedes. The car skewed and ran into the six-foot-thick earth safety-bank designed to function as an exterior brake and divert the driver back on to the track. This time, however, the reverse happened. The earth bank seemed to lift the car into a somersault so that it soared rocket-like into the air, somersaulted again before falling among the spectators, bounced once more and finally exploded into white-hot component parts, like shrapnel from an anti-personnel bomb.

Those few moments brought for many the instant eternity of death, including the driver himself whose body, thrown from the disintegrating car, was found dead near the roadside.

The shock was immediate but localized, and it is quite likely that only a tiny proportion of the crowd realized that anything at all had happened. It was, perhaps, to isolate those near the scene of death and destruction – a relatively small area – that the *gendarmes* moved in to set up a human barrier that could be penetrated only by doctors, firemen and professionally qualified helpers to speed up rescue work. For the same reason, perhaps, the decision was made at a high level to let the show continue – race, music and amusements.

The media were quickly on the spot and the disaster was soon being reported from every angle by international journalists, radio, television and newsreel men. To call it a field-day would be a misnomer; indeed, some film and television reports were so sickening that astonished producers and film editors, despite their love of the sensational, found themselves obliged to make cuts and fades. Even the printed word had to be moderated in many newspapers.

According to one reporter, 'the engine and back axle of the Mercedes sliced like a razor through the packed

Previous pages : The moment of impact. Police rush to the scene as a Mercedes taking part in the famous Le Mans race somersaults the protecting earth bank and explodes among the spectators.

The carnage among the spectators lining the race track was appalling. The scene was described by one reporter as being 'like a bloodstained battlefield. Women's screams rose above the roar of cars as they continued round the course'.

spectators. Some were decapitated, and for 100 yards along the straight the scene was like a bloodstained battlefield. Wailing men and women tried frantically to find out whether their friends or relations were among the victims. Women's screams rose above the roar of the cars as they continued round the course.'

A seasoned cameraman commented: 'I've covered wars and just about every type of horror job you can think of, but the stuff I've got here in the can is so appalling that it would make people sick to see it. There are kiddies with their heads sliced off – and their hands still gripping the ice-cream cornets they'd been sucking only seconds before. There was one father, mad with grief, refusing to believe that his son was dead and trying to carry him away to safety . . .'

Bodies lay everywhere. Many died en route to hospital. Ironically, those already dead were grotesquely covered with torn-down advertisement banners. Many had been charred by the fuel-fed flames of the Mercedes, whose engine contained a high proportion of weight-saving magnesium – an element well known for its explosive inflammability. Like an incendiary bomb, it defied the firemen and simply burned itself out.

Two English doctors worked alongside their French colleagues at the death site, although they had gone to Le Mans merely to see the race. With the approach of night came rain and a new crisis. The local hospital at Le Mans, after carrying out more than 80 transfusions, was rapidly running out of blood supplies. More was needed – much more – and urgently.

For the first time since the tragedy, the fairground music was silenced while doctors used the loudspeaker system to make urgent appeals for blood donors. There was no lack of response. Donors queued at waiting ambulances, then, having given blood, went back to watch the race which was still in progress, or to the funfair stalls which were still open for business.

Overcynical? Who can say? Perhaps it was the emotive reaction of the time, but on the other side of the coin the deliberate continuation of the race and funfair avoided possible chaos and obstruction to the essential rescue work in progress. The effect of a quarter of a million visitors trying to leave the ground at the same time can well be imagined.

The competitors themselves were obliged to drive lap after lap around the floodlit track when all of them wished to withdraw from what had become a fiasco. It was now a race in which there could be no true winner, but the sponsors were divided in their reactions. Mercedes, taking a very firm line, desperately tried to contact the firm's directors at Stuttgart for permission to pull out their cars, but the telephone lines were frantically busy and communication was subjected to long delays. In the end the West German Federal Government at Bonn intervened. Although the Le Mans organizers wanted the Germans to continue, at 1.45 a.m. on the Sunday the German team manager, Alfred Neubauer, received authority to flag in his two remaining cars which were running first and third, with Britain's Mike Hawthorn lying between.

The head of Jaguar, Mr William Lyons, also debated the abandonment of the race, but circumstances were rather different; his own son had been killed while driving a Jaguar to watch the race. He said, 'I can imagine nothing further from my son's wishes,' adding,

Wreaths mark the spot where the victims died, while the curious or the sympathetic come to gaze at the scene of the tragedy.

Among the debris of wreckage from the crashed car and the belongings of the victims, a priest helps in the rescue of the dead and injured. In a matter of seconds 82 people were killed and a hundred more seriously hurt.

without reference to the Mercedes withdrawal, 'racing in that respect is like flying. The risks are acknowledged and respected. But how can we be other than very grieved when a tragedy of this magnitude shadows the sport?'

The 1955 Le Mans Grand Prix was won, if the word has any meaning in retrospect, by Britain's Mike Hawthorn at an average speed of just over 107 m.p.h. He commented after the event: 'It was the one time in my career I'd have been equally glad to lose.'

Hawthorn was naturally the target for criticism, especially in France, for it was his move into the pit that had triggered the subsequent horror. In press correspondence it was alleged that he had failed to give the requisite hand signal to warn the following drivers of his intended move, and that he had misjudged the distance to his pit, overshooting it by some 80 yards. Both Macklin and Fangio echoed these criticisms some years later, although Hawthorn had been exonerated in the official inquiry following the disaster. Perhaps only Hawthorn himself knew the full truth, but he was killed a few years later (1959) in an ordinary road accident.

The French Government wasted no time in taking action. First, all motor racing was banned until new safety rules had been agreed and established. Second, after due deliberation, the new proposed safety regulations were put forward for international agreement.

Three main points emerged. The first was a ban on all racing events in which both high- and low-powered cars could compete simultaneously (it had been concluded that the relatively slow speed of Lance Macklin's Austin-Healey, hit by the much faster Mercedes, had been largely responsible for the catastrophe). Secondly, it was recommended that public stands on the course should be moved further away from the track, so reducing, if not totally eliminating, hazards to spectators. Finally, the pits, where cars were fuelled and maintained, should be moved over to a special side track well away from the public stands. These changes were internationally accepted and duly put into effect.

Lewisham, 1957

The cause of the rear-end collision near Lewisham, London, which killed 90 people on 4 December 1957 – the third worst death-toll in British railway history, exceeded only by Quintinshill and Harrow – was extremely simple: the driver ran through signals.

There were, of course, extenuating circumstances. It was a foggy night and, because of late running and delayed movements of stock in the London area, the driver and fireman on the 4.56 p.m. express from Cannon Street to Ramsgate did not have time to take on water during turn-around time, so the engine was being 'nursed' until the first passenger stop at Sevenoaks, Kent.

The engine was a Battle-of-Britain class Pacific No. 34066 Spitfire; and from London Bridge on the down fast line this express was following the 5.18 p.m. suburban electric train from Charing Cross to Hayes (Kent). There were drifting fog-banks over the south-eastern suburbs that evening, and the bulging rush-hour trains were groping their way out of London.

These are the most densely packed lines in the world with the possible exception of Tokyo – it was estimated at the period of the accident that a total of 990 trains passed St Johns signal-box at Lewisham every 24 hours. The box also controlled traffic on the Nunhead-Lewisham loop, which crosses over the Kent coast main line on a steel lattice-girder bridge at this point. This traffic increased the total to 1,115 trains a day.

There is no manual block working, traffic being governed by four-aspect automatic or semi-automatic colour-light signals controlled by continuous track-circuiting. The semi-automatic signals are operated from the signal-boxes, but when this control was exercized by the signalmen in acceptance of a train, they would only clear to the aspect dictated by the state of the track circuits: double-yellow, yellow or green as the case may be.

Double-yellow (YY) means that the driver may expect to find the next signal at single-yellow, an indication which means that the signal after that may be at red. Thus adequate braking distance between trains is

On a dark, foggy winter evening an express train, over an hour late, ran through danger signals and crashed into the back of a local electric train, packed with commuters, bringing down a viaduct on to the rear coaches of one of the trains. Ninety people died.

always maintained. There were 19 of these four-aspect signals in the five miles of line from Cannon Street to Parks Bridge Junction where the mid-Kent line diverged from the old South-eastern main line to Dover and Ramsgate. There were only two signal-boxes within this five miles – St Johns and North Kent East Junction.

The relevant signals are to the right of the line, while the Pacific was driven from the left of the foot-plate and had a special narrow cab for the Kent Coast line. It proved difficult, though not impossible, for the driver to see the signals in fog from his side of the foot-plate, with his close-up view being cut off by the streamlined bulk of the boiler-casing.

The fireman read the signals until the train was approaching St Johns outer and intermediate home signals; because these signals are on the outside of a left-hand curve they were normally within the driver's view and, for this reason, the fireman had no further need to look out, but began firing in readiness for the long climb to the summit of the North Downs at Knockholt.

But the driver did not see these two signals, nor did he cross the foot-plate to do so. Asked at the later inquiry why, having missed them, he failed to slow down, he could only reply that he had never experienced a signal check at this point. But this time the signals were showing a double-yellow and a yellow indicator respectively.

The fireman noticed the St Johns home signal and shouted to his driver: 'You've got a Red!', whereupon the driver at once made emergency application of the vacuum brake. Too late – 138 yards beyond the signal the Pacific crashed into the rear of the 5.18 p.m. Charing Cross-Hayes 10-coach electric train which was standing at the Parks Bridge Junction home signal. They telescoped upwards on to a viaduct and brought a 530-ton mass of steel girders roaring down on top of the wreckage – just as a third train was crossing the bridge...

Only by a fluke was a much greater disaster averted – the third train was derailed as the wrecked coaches shattered the viaduct and the driver stopped within inches of the edge. His train hung poised over the lip of the bridge, saved only by its couplings from a headlong plunge to the death and injury of hundreds more passengers. So threatening was the situation that police roused families living next to the line at 2 a.m. next morning and warned them to get ready to evacuate their homes in case the bridge heeled over down the embankment. Meanwhile, a 45-ton crane was ordered to the scene to pull the third train off the damaged bridge, which was canting over at nearly 45 degrees.

The most dramatic interview after the crash was given to reporters by Harry Chadwick, a 45-year-old window cleaner, who rescued 15 people from one carriage and helped to bring out 10 dead. 'I saw the wrecked coaches and heard screaming', he said. 'I climbed a five-foot fence and dashed up the embankment to see what I could do. I didn't bother watching out for the live lines. One carriage was tilted at an angle so I went underneath it as I heard screams coming from there.

'The first person I saw must be the bravest girl I have ever met. She was about 25 and her legs were smashed

The steel frame of the flyover resting on one of the wrecked coaches in which about 50 people lost their lives. Only by a fluke was a greater disaster averted. A third train crossing the bridge was derailed as the viaduct shattered, and the driver stopped within inches of the edge; the engine poised over the lip of the bridge was saved only by its couplings.

to the bone... Although in obvious pain she was smiling and worrying only about her husband who wouldn't know where she was. The sight of her legs was horrible. I tried to joke with her. She was surrounded by dead and one or two barely alive people who were moaning in the huddle. I had to be careful who I rescued because each time someone moved it hurt someone else as they were so squashed together.

'This girl was weighed down and twisted around other people... Gently and slowly I moved someone's arm and someone's leg, someone's head, someone's shopping-bag to get her free. All this time her face was wincing with pain. Eventually I got her free and it was only then I realized that the force of the crash had pushed her and the rest of the people in her compartment down through the floor on to the sleepers. To comfort her I assured her that her legs would be all right.

'About 10 minutes later I came on a little boy aged about three. He lay dead with his little tin drum lying on his tummy.'

Alongside the dead were strewn handbags, gloves, shoes, coats – and gaily wrapped Christmas parcels. There was an almost continuous procession of stretchers along the track to the assembly point for ambulances at St Johns station. The dead were laid alongside the track. So heavy was the casualty roll that there were not enough ambulances. Many victims had to be carried away laid out on wrenched-off compartment doors. Nearly every home in the district helped to treat the injured – blankets and bandages were willingly provided and tea made non-stop.

In the dense fog and ghostly glare of the floodlights the railway line presented a scene of horror. On the stretchers silk-stockinged feet peeped from beneath

coats and blankets. Gashed limbs and bodies added to the ghastly spectacle.

Police loudspeakers kept broadcasting urgent messages for doctors from a number of hospitals to return to the railway track as soon as possible to treat more injured. As rescue workers stumbled along the line in the swirling fog, a cry was heard: 'Watch out – the engine may explode!'

The stunned crew of the engine worked for an hour carrying bucketfuls of damp earth from the embankment side which they poured into the fire-box of the 120-ton locomotive to put out the fire. At 10.30 p.m., more than four hours after the crash, London Fire Brigade still had around 100 men on the spot with 15 appliances helping with the rescue work. By then all the dead and injured had been removed from the electric train and work was concentrated on the viaduct and the steam train. The wrecked engine lay across crushed coaches, its nose almost in the track cinders, its cabin many feet in the air.

Scores of passengers were trapped in the wreckage. All available police in the area were mobilized, vans were commandeered to help in the rescue work, acetylene lighting was brought by the fire brigade in an attempt to penetrate the fog, logs were fired to be used as flares.

The inquiry into the disaster was held on 12 December 1957, and was told that the speed of the Pacific train was estimated at between 35 and 40 m.p.h. Fog had cut visibility down to five yards in some areas, witnesses said. William John Trew, 61-year-old driver of the Pacific, did not attend the official inquiry – he was still at his home in Ramsgate suffering from shock. His fireman, Cyril Hoare, was also too ill to attend; he was in Lewisham hospital suffering from hip injuries and shock.

The casualty list totalled 90 dead, 109 seriously hurt and 67 slightly hurt. There were 770 passengers in the Pacific and 1,480 in the electric train. The bridge over the lines was brought down by the crash and 49 of the dead in the steam train were killed by the bridge collapse. Motorman J. B. Skilton, the driver of the Hayes electric train which was hit, was asked by Lieutenant Colonel G. R. S. Wilson, Transport Ministry Chief Investigation Officer, if he felt much of the crash. He replied: 'No, I felt a jolt. When I saw the scene it was much worse than I first thought.'

Colonel Wilson told the inquiry that he had made three journeys on the foot-plate of a Battle-of-Britain class locomotive – similar to the one Mr Trew was driving – to see line conditions for himself. 'I decided straight away that the speed could not have been less than 30 m.p.h. That was my guess from what I saw.'

How about visibility? The driver of a London Cannon Street–Hastings steam train, which passed through just before the crash, said he had a red and saw

Far right : Twenty-four hours after the disaster rescuers and workmen were still hard at work clearing the debris and bringing out the dead and seriously injured. Nearly every home in the area helped to treat the injured and provide blankets, tea and bandages.

Right : This photograph was taken inside one of the less seriously wrecked coaches, after it had been removed to a siding.

it between 35 and 40 yards away. Could he see the signals from his left-hand-drive cab? The driver replied: 'All signals were on the right-hand side of the engine. There is no difficulty in seeing them in clear weather, but in fog you could lose them with your engine obstructing them.'

And this is as near as we are likely to get to the truth of the matter; if the driver of the ill-fated express had crossed the foot-plate he should have seen the warning signals. It is in such seemingly small actions that so often lies the difference between a routine journey and a tragedy.

In his final word on Lewisham, Brigadier Langley stressed that the lesson of this crash should be borne in mind when new or replacement over-line bridges were designed, but above all he emphasized that the Lewisham disaster, like the previous one at Harrow and Wealdstone on 8 October 1952 (which had cost 122 lives), would have been prevented by some form of the Automatic Warning System (now in general use) at the distant signal point.

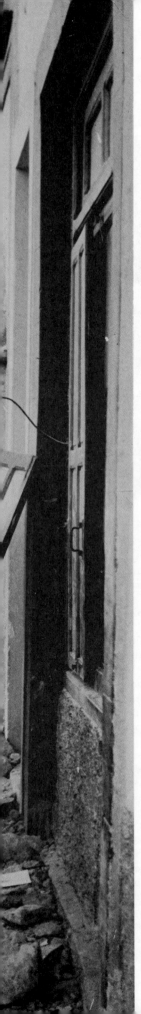

Agadir, 1960

To the people of Agadir and to the several thousand tourists enjoying its winter sunshine, 2 March 1960 had been just another day. Now, half an hour to midnight and with a high, bright moon looking down on the drowsy city enveloped in the warm clinging darkness of a Moroccan evening, that day was almost over.

In the big, modern hotels near the sea, the lights were going out one by one. The children, tired from a day's ceaseless activity on the magnificent beaches of golden sand and from the continuous excitement of new sights and sounds, had long been asleep. Many of their elders had followed their example, tired from another day of continual sunshine, of excursions to the four-centuries-old Casbah, and of an orgy of writing 'Having a wonderful time, wish you were here' postcards to less fortunate friends who were combating the chill of winter.

Some, of course, remained very much awake. The popular bar at the huge Saada Hotel, just off the main sea-front, still had its fringe of dedicated drinkers; the card salon of nearby Gauthier's had its nightly collection of bridge players who rarely looked up from their cards or score-sheets to gaze out across the hotel's boasted 'panoramic view of the bay'. Away from the hotel area, some of the tourists were sampling the more dubious pleasures of the mainly Muslim quarter of the Talbordj lying to the north-west, where cabarets with a 'native' flavour, including the commercialized exotic dances of old Morocco, had their admiring semi-circles of European patrons. Otherwise the whole city was still.

A casual talking point had been three earth tremors that had shaken the city during the week, but they had been so slight that they had passed almost unnoticed, although some of those at the Saada bar had wittily suggested that their duty-free drinks had more of a 'kick' than usual.

But those tremors had been a promise of more to come.

At 11.39 p.m. there came a fourth, a shock which lasted for nearly 10 whole seconds – an unusually long time – to become the worst earthquake tremor ever recorded in Morocco. The whole of the city and the surrounding countryside trembled and shook with the immeasurable power of that subterranean movement. That comparatively brief moment of time seemed an eternity to everyone in Agadir that night. To many it seemed like the end of the world. To several thousand it *was* the end of their world.

At 11.40 p.m. the moon illuminated a scene of utter, terrifying chaos. The great ultra-modern hotels that had been built to satisfy the demand of the post-war

A woman's face of anguish reflects the emotions of the people of Agadir after the terrifying earthquake.

tourist boom had suddenly become grotesque heaps of shapeless, dust-covered rubble. Every street was now littered with great piles of stones, masonry and plaster that had spilled across them, to block nearly every road from the shoreline to Talbordj where, a few moments before, many multi-storied blocks of flats had been silhouetted against the night sky. Now they, too, lay in piles of utter ruin. Only one road to this quarter was still open, and that had a huge gaping crack right across it.

As the rumbling and crashing came to an end, a ghastly screaming and shouting arose which developed into hysterical pandemonium as the survivors began to claw their way free of masonry and stones. Agadir had almost ceased to exist; even the ancient Casbah was destroyed, only a few dazed inhabitants, grey with dust and shock, groped their way from the ruins that had been their homes to stagger, shaking and sobbing, across the high pile of masonry that had formerly been the protecting wall to reach the fresh air and comparative quiet of the countryside.

With every line of communication cut, it was some time before news of the extent of the disaster was received in the French naval and air base which was still at Agadir (although France had recognized Morocco as an independent kingdom some four years earlier), but little could be done until dawn except alert other cities throughout the country, asking for urgent aid.

Dawn revealed an almost unbelievable sight. Nearly every hotel had been flattened, while damage in the thickly-populated Talbordj quarter had been as much as 90 per cent and some 80 per cent in the 'new town' nearby. Wherever the rescue teams looked they saw ruins with parked cars now shattered and half-buried with masonry. In some hotels, walls had crumbled away to reveal beds, some still sheltering the bodies of unfortunates who had been crushed in their sleep, hanging precariously and almost obscenely from the parapets of tottering walls, while the terrible screaming and moaning of the trapped or cries for help in a variety of languages rose on all sides.

The airport had escaped damage and was turned into a clearing house for the casualties. Aircraft began to arrive to carry the injured to Marrakesh, Rabat, and other cities which had escaped the effects of the earthquake, although Mogador, 100 miles to the north, had also suffered some damage from the fringes of the earthquake.

A group of sailors was put to work on what had been the imposing Saada Hotel. They struggled desperately against time, their uniforms dusty and torn, but for the most part they only uncovered the crushed bodies of tourists and hotel staff. Even so, they had some success. One group heard the voice of a child calling for its mother, apparently coming from deep below a huge mound of stones that had previously formed part of the

Top: French troops digging in the rubble to rescue a fifteen-year-old boy who was trapped, with only his head and one arm exposed, for over 30 hours.

Above: A general aerial view of the ruins of Agadir, which was destroyed by an earthquake on 2 March 1960. Ten thousand people are said to have died in the city.

façade of the hotel. They dug down, first with spades and picks and then, more gently, with bare hands, until they came upon the child, miraculously alive, trapped in a slight hollow beneath great stones and beams.

But that was to be one of their few successes, for out of the hotel's guest-list of more than 150, only 20 survived.

There was no electricity to light up darkened holes beneath the rubble that might shield a body and no water to dampen the flames which licked at shattered woodwork. Initially, every effort was devoted to finding and then removing the injured to safety and quickly burying the dead to avoid the risk of infection – always a danger to the living in tropical climates. Three thousand men of the Moroccan army were rushed to Agadir and then sent to patrol the whole area where the earthquake had also caused much damage. In the Moorish town of Inezgane, some seven miles away, damage was estimated at 30 per cent of the buildings.

A French naval squadron including an aircraft-carrier arrived off the coast; Dutch and Spanish warships joined it; Britain sent aircraft from Gibraltar to land at Agadir's airport. Soon a fleet of some 80 aircraft was operating a shuttle service to airlift the injured. More than 2,000 people were thus evacuated.

There was a number of British tourists in Agadir's hotels, and all of those who survived had alarming stories to tell. Alan Birtles of Warwickshire, for example, recalled that he and his wife were asleep in bed when there was a frightful rushing noise and a lot

they got to her.'

At the end of that first day the authorities ordered the complete evacuation of Agadir, then sealed off the whole area except for essential services. The Crown Prince of Morocco held a Press Conference to announce that the death-roll had risen to 10,000. That figure included 4,000 dead already found, with an estimated 6,000 still buried beneath the ruins. Some 20,000 people had escaped unhurt, he said, and the 2,000 injured had already been evacuated. Final figures were never accurately established, and other sources quoted widely differing statistics.

The rescue work went on, although by now it had developed into a search for bodies. So much quicklime had been scattered about to prevent infection that one observer said that parts of the city resembled snow-covered fields.

Yet there were miraculous survivals. On 9 March, a week after the earthquake, three Moroccans were rescued quite unscathed. A father and his 10-year-old son had been dug out alive and rescue workers began to search around the same area until, led by weak cries, they found another man. On the following day, eight more were rescued. Rescue workers listening and calling among the débris were answered by feeble cries on 11 March and during that day they dug out a man of 24, three women and a family of three Jewish children, two girls and a boy of six. The following day two more were rescued, one a 28-year-old Muslim, the other, as it happened, the father of the three children rescued the previous day. The two girls, Alice and Jacqueline Kalfon, related how they had told stories and sung to their little brother Armand during their ordeal beneath the débris of their house. All were rushed to hospital, where Armand died a few hours later.

Rescue work was also going on in the remote areas of the Atlas Mountains where nearly 600 were reported dead and more than 2,000 homeless.

Helicopters circling over the devastated areas reported that in some instances the ground had opened like giant jaws and swallowed villagers 'by the dozen'.

The earthquake had a strange effect upon the Atlantic coastline and seabed which made an extensive hydrographic survey essential. At one place where the water had been charted at 1,200 feet, soundings showed that it was now only 45 feet. This was not only inshore; for nine miles from the coastline soundings showed a depth of 1,200 feet instead of the previous 4,500 feet.

of crashing and screaming. It was pitch dark, which made matters worse. He tried the bedside light but the electricity cables had been ruptured. As he and his wife lurched about the room they found that the earthquake had brought all the drawers tumbling from the furniture, and they soon realized that plaster from the ceiling overhead was still falling about them. He managed to find a cigarette-lighter and by its meagre light they struggled into some clothes. Then, going to the door, they found it had jammed and they had to break it down before they could escape. 'We broke down the doors of other rooms in the corridor to help people out', he concluded.

Richard Waddington who had been staying at the Marhaba Hotel, one of the few large buildings that had not collapsed completely, stated that the most awful thing about the disaster was 'the terrible screaming and shouting from people trapped under the rubble; but you could not do anything about it.' He went on: 'I was fortunate, I suppose, because I was under only six feet of rubble and they got me out in six hours. My father was 16 feet down. It took 22 hours to free him. My mother was farther down still. She was dead when

The upper storey of a house in the Arab quarter of Talbordj stands almost intact, despite the fact that most of the ground floor has collapsed.
In this quarter damage was about 90 per cent, and the famous Casbah was destroyed.

Right: There were miraculous survivals, people being dug alive from the ruins as long as ten days after the disaster. This three-year-old girl was believed to be dead until she stirred and cried out for her mother.

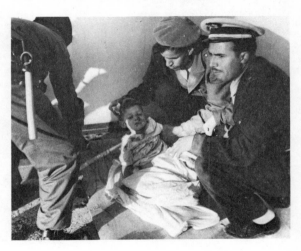

Mid-Air Collision, New York, 1960

It was mid-morning in New York on Friday, 16 December 1960, the last shopping weekend before Christmas. Heavy grey clouds hung over the city and wind-scattered flakes of sleet made shoppers snuggle deeper into their furs and topcoats. Nevertheless, in Manhattan, especially on Park and Fifth Avenues where the dazzling displays of such as Macys and Gimbels were drawing large crowds into their stores, business was brisk.

On the other side of the East River, however, across the Brooklyn Bridge, the streets were almost deserted. In Brooklyn itself, around the Park Slope area, there were as yet few seasonal displays for this was a run-down neighbourhood. Even so, a few Christmas wreaths had already made their appearance on doors and in windows along Sterling Place although, as yet, there were few about to appreciate them. It was just after 10.30 a.m., a time when the men had gone to work and children to school, while housewives and the elderly were mainly indoors, for the dismal weather did not encourage anyone leaving the comparative comfort of their homes.

Soon after 10 o'clock, Jo Colacano and John Opperisano arrived and began to set up some Christmas trees, sticking their sawn butts into a dirty snow-bank opposite a vacant Sterling Place store. Nearby, Charles Cooper, a sanitary worker, was content to lean upon his snow shovel and watch them. For a moment in time the two salesmen and their silent onlooker existed; the next they were completely obliterated.

For out of the morning murk came a blazing airliner which sliced the steeple off the tall, sombre building of the Pillar of Fire Church, then buried itself in the church's foundations, bringing its wall down on top of it and destroying a funeral parlour at the same time, while its tailplane, burning furiously, spun over and over as it bounced along the street. A few moments before, the gutters had been brimming with brown slush. Now they were suddenly filled with blazing rivulets of jet fuel which, racing down the slope of Sterling Place, enveloped parked cars with flame, setting off a chain of smaller explosions as the gasoline tanks were ignited. Within minutes a six-storey tenement building, some shops and offices were blazing furiously. Wreckage was suddenly spread over a square mile, causing a holocaust of fire and ruin that brought brigades dashing to the devastated area from all over Brooklyn and Manhattan.

The crashed aircraft was a United Airlines DC8 jetliner which had been approaching New York from Chicago, with 77 passengers and a crew of seven. It had been due to touch down at Idlewild (now Kennedy) Airport at 10.45 a.m.

Firemen arrived on the scene of disaster where a series of explosions was igniting roofs and spraying further wreckage in all directions. A few moments after the plane had crashed women, children and elderly persons came pouring from the tenements into the street, dressed in a bizarre variety of sweaters, housecoats and even pyjamas. They were still running in aimless panic beneath a canopy of dense black smoke when the first of the brigades arrived. Any rescue work, so far, had been impossible for as one witness said: 'The heat was terrific and the flames were shooting three

Left : Death fell hideously from the sky to land in Brooklyn. The tailplane and wing of the United Airlines DC8 jet airliner, was involved in a mid-air collision with a Lockheed Super Constellation.

Right : A general view of the devastation. The blazing DC8 sliced the steeple off a church, then buried itself in the church's foundations, bringing a wall down on top of it while the burning tailplane somersaulted down the street.

stories high. We couldn't get near the place, so we helped people out of threatened houses,' significantly adding, 'We heard no screams from the wreckage.'

As the firemen began to move in a miracle happened; a small boy was seen crawling through a hole in the fiercely blazing fuselage. He was Stephen Baltz, an 11-year-old, flying alone to Idlewild to be met by his mother and to spend the Christmas with her. His clothing was on fire, but he was seized and rolled in the snow until the flames were extinguished. Then, as he was carried away, a fireman cradling him gently in his arms, the boy asked, weakly, 'What happened?' before lapsing into unconsciousness.

Although it was a seven-alarm fire, involving 250 firemen and more than 50 pieces of equipment, it took more than two hours to bring the raging fire under control.

At almost the same time as the Brooklyn disaster, another plane crashed at one end of a small army air force strip, known as the Miller Army Air Field, on Staten Island, some 11 miles to the south-west. Unlike the Douglas DC8 which was jet-powered, this machine, a Lockheed Super Constellation, was a four-engined turbo prop aircraft. It was a Trans World airliner bound from Dayton and Columbus, Ohio, to La Guardia airfield with 39 passengers and a crew of five. Its estimated time of arrival was 10.40 a.m. An eye-witness described what happened: 'I saw the engine on the right side blow up. I only saw one plane . . . then the second engine on the right side blew up and when it did it blew the tail section to pieces. I saw a couple of people falling out of the plane. It was on fire from the time it blew up to the time it crashed.'

A 30-foot section of wing and an engine landed about 50 feet from a row of officers' frame quarters at the end of the field, but unlike the other disaster in Brooklyn, no one on the ground was injured. As the rear half of the plane's fuselage swirled out of the heavy overhang to smash into the earth it split open 'like a huge silver lobster shell'.

A Roman Catholic priest had his own version of what had happened. 'I looked up and saw the Constellation coming in towards Miller Field. It seemed under control. Suddenly there was an explosion, one wing fell off and the plane plunged to the ground.'

Above : Bodies of victims lie on the pavement close to the still flaming wreckage of the United Airlines jet which crashed into the street. Miraculously, only six people were killed.

None of the eye-witnesses realized that more than one aircraft was involved, none reported seeing two planes collide in mid-air, and the first editions of the newspapers suggested that the DC8 had crashed while attempting to land and the Constellation had exploded in mid-air and crashed on Staten Island. But the realization that the T.W.A. plane had fallen in three parts on the Island revealed that it could not have broken up after hitting the ground; and then, among its wreckage, an unmistakable jet engine was found.

Within minutes of the crash, fire-engines were at the scene and soon smothered the fiercely burning forward section with foam. One hundred firemen and nearly as many off-duty firemen were on the spot; they quickly quenched the fire and then began to pull the wreckage apart with winches and crowbars. There were no survivors. The firemen lifted out body after body, placing them in long even rows and then covering them with olive drab army blankets brought by servicemen from their quarters at the other end of the field.

The report that bodies had been seen falling from the plane as it plunged earthwards sent a fleet of Coast Guards' boats searching hopefully for survivors in the icy waters of the river and sea. Six were found but none survived the shock of their immersion.

Two off-duty policemen, brothers named Peter and Gerard Paul, were near the crash and immediately rushed to the rear section of the plane. 'We were the

first ones there. I got out a knife and began trying to cut the people free from their safety-belts. We counted nine passengers. It was very quiet.'

Although there was some initial confusion on the ground, the men of both approach control towers at La Guardia and Idlewild were all too horribly aware of what had happened. The United Airlines jet had been ordered by traffic controllers to fly a holding (or stacking) pattern 5,000 feet above Preston, New Jersey, until it was given the clear to proceed to Idlewild. At the same time the T.W.A. plane was directed to fly a similar holding pattern 6,000 feet over La Guardia. Their separate courses from the holding pattern to either airport would be several miles apart. While radar screen operators at both airfields stood almost hypnotized, they saw the images of the two aircraft merge into one and continue for a short distance, until one broke free of the other and fell away out of sight.

A few days after the accident, experts made test flights along the approaches to the New York area and were satisfied that there was nothing wrong with the radio navigation equipment used at both airfields or with their traffic control procedure. They later reported that the disaster was one of human error, for there was a buffer zone of at least three miles between the two holding areas for Idlewild and La Guardia. It was also agreed that the DC8 jet airliner was off-course, it had left its position and, by blundering into the other zone, had collided with the Constellation as it was about to make its approach run for La Guardia.

The only survivor from the New York crash, little Stephen Baltz, recovered consciousness and had given the only first-hand account of the crash. 'I remember looking out of the plane window at the snow below covering the city. It looked like a picture out of a fairy book. It was a beautiful sight. Then, suddenly, there was an explosion. The plane started to fall and people started to scream. I held on to my seat and then the plane crashed. That's all I remember.'

He became unconscious again soon afterwards, and although a team of eight doctors and twelve nurses worked around the clock to save his young life, they were unsuccessful. His lungs had been destroyed by the fumes and flames he had breathed in as he had crawled to safety, and although he fought for life with great bravery, there was no hope. His father spoke his epitaph. 'Stevie tried awfully hard, because he was a wonderful boy.'

The loss of life, 134 persons composed of 128 passengers (including three babies-in-arms) and crews, and six persons on the ground, was the world's worst air disaster up to that time.

There were several strange coincidences in connection with this New York crash. The worst air disaster to date had also involved the same two companies, United Airlines and T.W.A., when two of their planes collided in mid-air over the Grand Canyon, Arizona.

Sir Edmund Hillary, the world-famous conqueror of Everest in 1951, was thought at first to have been on the DC8 from Chicago with two companions, but he had been unable to leave for the airport owing to last-minute pressure of work and the plane left without him: he even had the tickets in his pocket at the time.

The crash sparked off a large number of claims and litigation. One of the passengers carried more than

$500,000 worth of life insurance, six others had more than $450,000 worth between them. There were also suits against the United States Government and both airlines, totalling some $25 million. The inquiry, held in June 1962, put all the blame on the pilot and crew of the DC8, it having been established that at the moment of collision, this aircraft was nine miles off-course. A contributory factor, said the inquiry, was that the pilot had not throttled back when in the holding zone and had allowed his craft to continue at a speed of 346 miles per hour instead of the 200-odd miles per hour that was obligatory at a low level of 5,000 feet.

Yet how much worse the disaster might have been. The T.W.A. Super Constellation ploughed its way along a vacant airfield with no loss of life other than its unfortunate occupants. The DC8, ramming its blazing fuselage into a densely populated area of Brooklyn killed six persons on the ground, whereas the final total could so very easily have been much greater. Indeed, as the forepart of the plane neared the end of its death plunge it narrowly missed the St Augustine's Roman Catholic Church where some 1,700 pupils were at their desks, débris actually landing in the schoolyard. Looking later at the scene and realizing 'what might have been' a bystander exclaimed devoutly, 'God brought that plane in.'

This tragedy at Christmas-time which was to throw a shadow over the whole city, ended on a further tragic and unusual note. Learning of the New York disaster, President Luebke of West Germany sent a cable to America's President Eisenhower to express his country's sympathy. Hardly had his message been received, however, than another disaster occurred in the West German city of Munich. Major-General Ernest Moore, Commanding Officer of the U.S. 3rd Air Force in Britain, had flown to Germany for Christmas leave. Not needing his plane over the weekend, he had allowed it to be used to fly home a dozen American students, sons and daughters of U.S. servicemen in Britain, who had been attending a University of Maryland extension course in Munich.

The plane, with a crew of seven, got out of control and crashed on to a street-car crowded with Christmas shoppers in the centre of Munich. Everyone died in the aircraft and 31 Germans were killed either in the car or in the street where the plane had crashed.

This was a sad ending to 1960, a year which had seen a record number of fatalities in U.S. schedule airlines – 388 persons in all – breaking the previous record of 294 of the previous year.

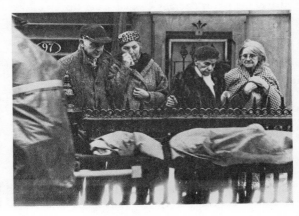

The Vaiont Dam, 1963

In the north-eastern corner of Italy, where the Italian Alps merge with those of Switzerland and Jugoslavia, there are many rivers which are the source of water and hydro-electric power for northern Italy. Across the valleys dams have been built and reservoirs created.

The Vaiont Dam formed part of a complex of five dams, which togetner made up the north-west-Piave hydro-electric scheme. When it was opened in 1960 it was the third highest concrete dam in the world, its wedge-shaped wall towering 873 feet above the Piave river and the valley below. In this valley, on the banks of the river, lay a number of small villages. Closest to the dam was Longarone, a village of less than 2,000 people, and a number of outlying hamlets.

The autumn of 1963 was unusually wet. Rain had loosened the rocks and earth of the mountain slopes which formed the shores of the reservoir. One of these, Mount Toc, which rises steeply to a height of 6,000 feet, had caused such apprehension that on 8 October a mayor in the district issued a warning to fishermen and others who might venture on the lake shores of the possibility of landslides causing dangerous waves.

Anybody who lives close to a dam is aware of the possibility of a fault and the disaster that could follow. The people in the district of Longarone were no exception, but they had no apprehension of danger on the night of Wednesday, 9 October 1963. At 11.00 p.m. they were all at home, either in bed or watching television. Fifteen minutes later a vast avalanche swept down the slopes of Mount Toc and thousands of tons of rocks, mud, earth and uprooted trees tumbled into the lake. The effect was that of throwing a large stone into a basin of water. Although the reservoir was by no means full it promptly overflowed, spilling over the top of the dam and pouring into the valley below.

The few survivors said later they heard that fearful sound which is so often described as the first intimation of disaster – a noise like thunder. They assumed at once that the dam had given way and, pausing only to gather up those nearest to them, they fled, but only the people whose houses lay close to the high ground at the edge of the valley had any chance. Over the lip of the dam poured a torrent of water, mud, rock and timber, creating a towering wall which swept along the valley below, swirled up the hillside and engulfed villages in a horrifying, overwhelming tide.

The natural assumption that both survivors and the authorities initially made – that the dam had burst – was not corrected until the dawn. The night had been chaos and pandemonium: the sun rose to reveal a macabre scene – a vast, silent desert of rock and mud and rubble, with here and there the remains of a building. Longarone, four-fifths destroyed, was a heap of stones; so were the nearby hamlets of Faè and Pirago, where all the inhabitants died. Two other hamlets, Codissago and Castellavazzo, lost half their population;

the two on the lake were wiped out, with three-quarters of the population missing.

It took time to establish these facts, for communications were destroyed. Telephone and telegraph lines were cut; railway lines turned and twisted in crazy spirals of buckled steel; and roads leading into the devastated villages were unidentifiable swamps. When the Italian Minister of Public Works visited the scene he described it as 'a truly biblical disaster . . . like Pompeii before the excavations began.'

With daylight came the first of the helpers, ploughing through the morass in the valley below the dam, where the river was swollen to twice its natural size by the waters pouring into it. Throughout the day bodies were washed up as workers struggled to reach the stricken villages in a frantic search for survivors. The final approaches to Longarone, now quagmires blocked with rubble and timber and the dead bodies of cattle, became choked with soldiers, ambulances, lorries and people desperately hoping for news of friends or relatives.

There was little hope for those who had not managed to escape to the high ground. The force of the great wave could be seen in the twisted pieces of metal, the total destruction, the bodies found hurled high into trees. The problem of extricating the bodies was immense: the municipal authorities at Belluno immediately ordered 500 coffins but as the days passed it became apparent that these would not be enough. Five days later rescuers were still digging for bodies and the problems of identification grew. Many were disfigured

Displaced by a huge fall of rocks, mud and trees from a neighbouring mountain, hundreds of tons of water poured over the top of the Vaiont Dam wall, sweeping everything before them and bringing wholesale destruction to the villages and towns which lay in the valley and at the side of the lake. It was described as 'a truly Biblical disaster'.

and denuded of clothing: whole families had died and there was nobody left to identify them. Eventually many were buried, unknown, although occasionally one of the thousands of helpers would find himself facing and able to identify someone he once knew.

The gruesome task was soon well organized. Bodies were extracted, sprayed with disinfectant, put in plastic shrouds and into simple coffins away from the warm sun as quickly as possible. A helicopter service was established and bodies arrived heaped on lorries, or carried, roughly-covered, on stretchers from the helicopters. The final death-toll totalled 1,189, although possibly some were not found. But on the morning of 12 October, two children were discovered, still alive, in the cellar under the débris of their home. While there was still hope of survivors, the rescue work continued at full intensity.

An urgent inquiry was made into the safety of the dam. It was inspected and found to have suffered only some damage to the top of its retaining wall. The vast extent of the landslide could be judged from the fact that little over a third of the original reservoir remained. Instead, a new mountain filled the centre of the dam, some grass and lopsided trees still covering its surface.

Almost immediately the cause of the disaster became a political issue and the subject of exhaustive inquiries. Rock-falls and small earth movements of the mountain were known to have occurred. The crucial question was: should a dam have been built in that situation in the first place? Three years after its completion it came to light that research was still being made into the suitability of its location.

A court of inquiry was set up to consider a number of questions and to establish whether the disaster could have been avoided. It had to consider various aspects: Was the location badly chosen? Was the dam badly designed? Was the area, and in particular the hazard constituted by the mountain, monitored frequently enough? Had the local authorities taken sufficient care in the warnings they issued? A minor earth tremor had

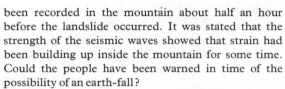

Above: In the morning after the disaster, rescue workers searched among the rubble of houses for the injured and brought them to a makeshift first-aid post.

Below: In Longarone, the village closest to the dam, rescue workers could do little but dig for bodies. The final death roll totalled 1,189.

been recorded in the mountain about half an hour before the landslide occurred. It was stated that the strength of the seismic waves showed that strain had been building up inside the mountain for some time. Could the people have been warned in time of the possibility of an earth-fall?

Although the court had been involved as a result of Communist pressure upon the Government whom they accused of negligence, it soon became apparent that there were grounds for such an inquiry; when its findings were eventually published there seemed little doubt that, with more care and more exhaustive enquiries into its potential dangers, the site would never have been chosen. The nationalized Italian electrical industry, which was responsible for the hydro-electric scheme, was found to be at fault. Builders and civil engineers were also found to carry some of the blame for a construction unsuitable to its particular site. It was common knowledge that there had been concern over the safety of the mountain. When the dam was being built and the reservoir filled, a series of landslides and cracks had appeared in the mountain, which had had to be reinforced with concrete to a depth of several feet on either side of the dam. Instruments recorded stresses and strains on the rock face, and the reservoir was not completely filled until two years after the dam had been completed. At the time of the flood all the men working at the dam were killed, but one who had worked on the original construction claimed that the technicians were waiting for such a disaster from one day to the next.

The local authorities, said the inquiry, must have known of this situation. Why did they do no more than warn the local inhabitants of the dangers on the lake itself? Some communities living around the lake and on Mount Toc had been evacuated. Should not the inhabitants of the valley also have been evacuated? Or at least warned of the possible dangers in strong terms?

As a direct result of the inquiry, the ill-conceived Vaiont Dam was closed down. The devastated villages were rebuilt and new factories sited in the valley.

The Mattmark Dam, 1965

Most people deplore any man-made construction which affects natural beauty and few of them enhance the scenery. Dams, however, are sometimes an exception. If the wall itself is attractive, once the reservoir is filled and its shores covered with grass, trees and undergrowth, the site can be very beautiful.

A dam under construction, however, is a far from beautiful sight. Dirt roads criss-cross the valley and curve round the hillsides; concrete-mixers, silos, stone-crushing plant and huge conveyor-belts are littered – apparently aimlessly – around the site. Where the dam itself is taking shape is an ugly concrete wall, the steel reinforcement rods protruding from its surface. On the valley floor are temporary huts – engineers' and contractors' offices, canteens, engine-sheds and stores; and, often, living quarters for the men, if the site is a long distance from any nearby town. All over the area is a ceaseless movement and a continuous roar from lorries, trucks, bulldozers, earth-moving plant and all the other mechanized equipment involved in a major civil-engineering project. Everywhere two or three hundred men are in constant activity as they go about their work.

In August 1965 the Mattmark Dam presented just such a scene of activity as it neared its final phase of construction. Situated in the Valais Alps in Western Switzerland and overshadowed by the 13,200-foot-high Allalin mountain, the dam was only a few miles from the skiing and mountaineering resort of Saas Fée, a popular place in both summer and winter. On the evening of 30 August a number of tourists and climbers in the area looked down upon 500 men – Italian, Spanish, Austrian and Swiss – at work upon the site while, in the canteen in the construction camp at the foot of the dam, some 60 men who were about to go on night shift were having their evening meal. One of the workers described what happened:

'I heard a roar and looked up towards the mountain and the glacier on its slopes. I saw a section come away from the foot of the glacier. The sound it made was even larger than the engine of my bulldozer. Some of the ice came within 10 feet of me. I saw a truck driven by a friend carry straight on into the course of the slide and disappear.'

Within seconds a part of the Allalin glacier had crashed 1,000 feet, sweeping away a score of trucks and three or four bulldozers and demolishing the camp at the foot of the dam, burying it in ice and rocks to a depth of 80 feet.

For long moments after the terrifying roar ceased and the valley was still again, those who had escaped gazed unbelievingly at the scene. Forty German and Swiss tourists had just been visiting the dam and were waiting to depart. The coach which was on its way to fetch them received a blast of air which rocked the heavy vehicle, while 50 yards in front of it a 30-ton

bulldozer was flung into the air before being engulfed, with its driver. Two Swiss tourists, a father and son, had, only a few minutes before, been refused a drink at the camp café, which was reserved for workers. They were not far away when the avalanche engulfed it. Now, where the camp had been, there was an incongruous sprawl of white against the grey of the dam and the mountain-slopes scarred with the tracks of bulldozers. The entire area below the dam was piled high with ice and rocks. The débris of a dormitory – beds, clothes, roof and floor – was thrown up on one side of the avalancne; heavy vehicles lay on their sides like toys. On top of one slab of rock stood a small car, its chrome gleaming in the setting sun, apparently undamaged.

Rescue work began at once. Excavators and bulldozers moved in, but the depth and weight of the ice made it impossible for them to do more than hammer at the edges of the avalanche and no more than a handful of bodies was recovered. Experienced rescue teams, police and helpers worked throughout the night and the next day, hoping to find some survivors trapped in a corner of a hut or in a lorry cab. But the evidence of twisted steel girders, which had once formed the frames of the camp huts, and shattered machinery showed that the weight of the ice had crumpled steel plate like tinfoil.

During the days that followed rescue work was continually being suspended for fear of further avalanches. Small landslides that threatened to start a larger one had workers running for cover. It was soon apparent that nobody could be alive under the ice, and relatives waiting at the main camp centre in the nearby village of Saas Amagal were told there was no more hope; and that it might take months to recover all the bodies.

Most of the workers on the dam were Italians, but among them were Swiss, Germans, Hungarians and other nationalities, whose relatives had travelled many miles to wait anxiously for news. The information that their husbands, fathers or brothers were certainly dead was bad enough; to be told that their bodies might remain under tons of ice and rock for many months before they could be decently buried was heartbreaking. They heard the news in stunned silence. For a while some relatives lingered on, in a vain, unreasoning hope. Finally they gave up and returned drearily home.

Everything was against the rescuers. Cloud, a chill wind and driving rain hampered their efforts. Work had to stop when guides reported that the glacier was still in motion. Work was suspended while helicopters dropped small, delayed-action bombs on the glacier in order to dislodge more ice – larger than the first avalanche – which now threatened the site. Rescue work was limited to a small area out of danger, and bodies were recovered slowly. Explosives, mortars and mine-throwers were used to dislodge some menacing icicles; but the unstable, threatening mass of ice remained, and fog and snow made the search even more difficult, while every now and then rescue workers had to run for their lives as rock-falls continued.

Three days after the avalanche only nine bodies had been recovered, although 89 men were missing. Bombs had failed to dislodge the menacing ice above the valley, and Alpine guides climbed the mountain to place high explosives. The weather improved and

recovery work continued – but the better weather brought its own dangers as the ice started to melt and a new collapse was feared.

And so the long, grim story continued. Six weeks later a total of 53 bodies had been found, and it was months before the recovery work ended. Meanwhile the local people were expressing their fears that the glacier had damaged the dam or that a fresh avalanche would occur. The tragedy of the Piave valley was still fresh in everyone's mind. Could the same thing happen here? And why had it ever occurred in the first place?

Scientists inspected the dam itself and pronounced it safe: work continued. As for the avalanche, a small earth tremor the week before was blamed for loosening the vast mass of ice; but there was no real evidence that this was so, and no watch had been put on the glacier which for months had menaced hundreds of men.

Avalanche protection, prevention and warning is a highly developed science in Switzerland, particularly in the resorts popular with skiers and climbers. Most avalanches are caused by special conditions of the snow and may be triggered off by nothing more than a careless, or unlucky, skier. A glacier is normally more stable – although it is, of course, vulnerable through the possible melting of the ice – and has the feature of a landslide rather than a snow avalanche.

It is easy to be wise afterwards, but at any rate it is now clear that a mountain such as the Allalin, which dominated a valley where hundreds of people were working, should have been the subject of continual monitoring to ensure that no danger was threatening. After the avalanche, the glacier and the mountain-side were closely watched, and at one time the valley in the area of the Mattmark Dam was completely closed for fear of further avalanches, In fact none took place, although minor landslides occurred and boulders continued to fall for many days after the disaster. Nobody, however, was hurt, for warnings were given of the instability of the rock and ice-face, and workers were kept out of the path of a possible slide. Such monitoring could have saved the lives of the workers at Mattmark.

The Swiss are also highly skilled and experienced at rescue work. As soon as an avalanche is reported anywhere in Switzerland, a team of scientists from the Davos Institute is mobilized. In addition, rescue teams from the Ski Association, the Alpine Club and the Air-Rescue are called up. The rescue teams of the first two organizations are equipped with long avalanche poles and specially trained avalanche dogs for finding buried victims. In the case of the Mattmark avalanche, ice and rock, not snow, had buried the victims and probing poles were useless. The rescuers used acoustic sounding apparatus to listen – in vain – for any sound of life. Such was the weight of the ice that there was not only little hope of survivors, there was also enormous difficulty in clearing the fall. Earth-moving equipment, bulldozers and other machinery had little effect on the concrete-hard ice, and eventually great pressure hoses were brought in to melt it.

As a result of the demands of the people of the villages below the Mattmark Dam, the dam itself and the neighbouring mountains are now continually surveyed. Warnings will be given if any danger is observed from failure of the dam or movement of the mountain or its glacier.

Turkey, 1966

Every year, throughout the world, there are more than 30,000 recorded earthquakes, but only about 20 per cent of those are felt by people in the affected area. Frequently, only the sensitive seismograph records the fact that there has been a vibration of the earth's crust. These earth tremors occur in all parts of the world, but about 90 per cent of them happen in two great regions. One is the belt surrounding the Pacific Ocean, the other is the mountain chain from the Alps through the Himalayas. Every one of these 30,000-plus tremors is classified, no matter how slight. The worst, judged by loss of life and/or damage to buildings, are termed catastrophic.

An earthquake that easily qualified for this classification devastated part of Turkey in 1966. It was to prove one of the worst earthquakes of all time, certainly since seismology became an exact science.

During Friday, 19 August 1966, the earth suddenly buckled and heaved in a catastrophic series of waves that swept across the Turkish provinces of Erzurum, Mus, Bingol and Bitlis in Eastern Anatolia near the borders of the Soviet Union, Iran and Iraq. The severest damage and the scene of the greatest loss of life was in the vicinity of Varto, west of Lake Van in Mus, about 450 miles east of Ankara, although throughout the four provinces the damage was considerable, some 140 villages being almost totally destroyed.

Varto itself had already had two tremors earlier in the year, one in March which had killed seven persons and another in July which took another 12 lives but now, shaken and riven by the colossal force of this new eruption, the town was left with hardly a building standing and with some 2,000 of its population of 28,000 dead. As is usual with earthquakes, the majority of the deaths were caused by falling buildings and not by the actual disturbance of the earth.

As soon as the news of the disaster was received, men of the Turkish army began to battle towards the disaster area, though for a time were able to make little progress. The roads, poor at the best of times – for the area is remote and primitive – were in many places impassable due to landslides and crevasses and the men had to make many time-consuming diversions. At last they reached Varto and, assisted by police and civilian volunteers, worked throughout the night. The men, digging frantically, had only flares and the cries of the trapped to guide them. They toiled on, extricating families from beneath the ruins of their shattered homes but all too often were met by the still white faces of the dead. Much of the work was done by soldiers from Turkey's 3rd Army Corps based at Erzurum, an ancient hill-top city of mosques and minarets which had also suffered considerably in the earthquake.

Work became easier with the dawn which revealed all

Left : Erzerum, an ancient hill-top city of mosques and minarets, had a population of 70,000 until one of the worst earthquakes of all time reduced it to a mass of rubble, giving it the appearance of a long-since abandoned city.

Far left : Within an hour or two of the earthquake rescuers were digging and probing for bodies in the remains of buildings which were largely constructed of clay and wattle. The Turkish army had a Brigade headquarters well outside the town, and troops were brought to join in the rescue work.

A mother is handed the body of her child, one of the many victims of the town of Varto, which took the full force of the earthquake. She has only a few minutes to wash the body and wrap it in cloth before it is taken to be buried.

Emergency hospitals and field kitchens were soon set up and the starving thousands were more adequately fed. A new threat now emerged: the danger of cholera. Water supplies and sewers had been shattered and wells ruptured or dried up. Great clouds of black flies were settling upon the ruins and the corpses being laid out by the roadside and covered with white bed-linen. A massive anti-cholera campaign was immediately put into operation, more than 200,000 people in the south-eastern provinces being vaccinated in two days – a remarkable achievement. The border with Iraq was closed and patrols on duty had orders to shoot anyone crossing into Turkey from that country who refused to be vaccinated.

National mourning was declared throughout the whole country. All official functions were cancelled, cinemas and night clubs were closed and newspapers printed their titles in black instead of the usual red. Suleiman Demirel, Turkey's Prime Minister, set off on a tour of the devastated areas, going from village to village by helicopter, although tremors were still occurring from time to time. When he arrived in Varto he found that Mustafa Kafanil, mayor of the town, was very angry. 'My people were left to look after themselves for hours when the town collapsed,' he said. 'Please send us picks and shovels so that we may dig for those still buried.'

Demirel promised to do what he could and moved on to the next devastated spot where he narrowly escaped death, for as he moved forward a wall behind him collapsed, crashing on to the spot where he had been standing a moment earlier.

In one village a woman rushed forward and grabbed his arm. 'I have lost three sons,' she sobbed, 'and my fourth child is still buried beneath the school. I could still hear him calling me today . . . please save my last child.' As Demirel turned to comfort her, however, he was cut short by a sudden tremor which made the ground heave and buckle beneath their feet. Most of the crowd which had surrounded him, including the unfortunate woman, ran off and were not seen again.

The vital rescue work went on, men of many nations now working side by side with the Turks. From England came a team of 20 Civil Defence workers, specially trained for such an emergency, who were sponsored by the Oxford Committee for Famine Relief. They were flown out three days after the eruption.

Horrific stories of personal tragedies were soon circulated to the world by eye-witnesses. In one village, a survivor carried the bodies of his wife and four children from his shattered home, washing and then burying them, refusing help offered by sympathetic soldiers. Instead of accepting their aid he pointed to a high mound of rubble which had formerly been a cinema. Following his urging, the troops began to clear the rubble to disclose perhaps the most pathetic incident in the whole terrible disaster. A children's film show had been in progress at the time of the earthquake and some 200 mothers and their children were found dead, many of the latter still cradled in their mothers' arms in a vain attempt to shelter them from the roof that had crashed down upon them. As the troops dug, one young peasant became hysterical with joy for her young daughter was recovered, still alive, after having been buried for 36 hours.

too clearly the terrible nature and extent of the disaster. There were about 2,000,000 people living in the surrounding villages and most of them, dreading new tremors or without homes, were preparing to camp out in the fields. The soldiers began to move into these villages, in some cases finding them virtually ghost towns, lifeless and desolate, with only heaps of rubble to mark where the houses of the peasants had stood. In some villages peasants erected makeshift tents on pathetic mounds of stones and timbers which had been their homes, as if reluctant to leave the one familiar spot where they had been born and raised.

By Sunday, 21 August, better-equipped rescue teams were getting through, carrying blankets and medical supplies; also a few lorries and trucks arrived with bread and melons for the ravenous people and with 15 Muslim priests who had been sent by the Government to conduct mass burials in the area.

Nearby an old man sat mourning in the rubble of his daughter's home. 'My grandson,' he moaned. 'Dead. And I did not even see him take his first steps.'

There were, of course, other incidents which had happier endings. When troops arrived in one village they found a farmer frantically searching among the ruins of his home. He had already discovered the bodies of his family and had buried them in a makeshift grave nearby, but had still not found his three-year-old son. He begged the soldiers to help him search, saying that he wanted to find the boy to give him a better burial, and several men were detached to help. As they dug, a trunk was unearthed and put to one side until, out of curiosity, one of the soldiers opened it. Curled up inside was the boy, alive, but starving and semi-conscious. The father's joyful shout brought other villagers hastening to the scene and they gathered round, praising Allah for such a deliverance.

When such moving accounts of the disaster reached Britain, the response was immediate. Five British charities joined together under one heading – Disaster Emergency Committee; they were War on Want, Save the Children Fund, Oxfam, Christian Aid and the British Red Cross. Immediate assistance was organized and sent, and an appeal raised more than £250,000 in less than a week. A tremendous amount of supplies were despatched from Britain and other European countries.

As part of its 'Food for Peace' programme, America dispatched $1.1 million in kind to Turkey and its 1966 allocation of aid ($160.2 million) to the country included $15.2 million in straight grants for assistance in emergencies.

A general distribution point for medicines, food and other relief supplies was set up at Varto, the community

which had been hardest hit. It was staffed by nearly 4,000 officers and men, with about 450 vehicles. However, a tremendous argument arose and finally all the relief supplies were taken over, to be handled and distributed by the Turkish Army, following charges in the press that certain civilians were using the supplies for political and personal gain.

The final death-toll was never established. Many bodies had disappeared without trace and so many others had been buried by relatives, that accurate figures were impossible. A conservative estimate was 2,500 dead and 1,500 injured.

Top: In Varto where nearly 2,000 people were crushed by falling buildings, people continued to sleep outside for many days.

Above: Aid was rushed to Turkey from all over the world and temporary camps were set up for the victims.

Aberfan, 1966

On 21 October 1966, the worst disaster of its kind ever to occur in Britain struck the village of Aberfan in South Wales. In a matter of seconds almost an entire generation of children perished under millions of tons of mine waste, rock and sludge, which came pouring down from a nearby tip to engulf the Pontglas Infants' and Junior School, a row of terraced cottages and a farm.

The 'flow slide', as it is called, of relatively dry material came down like an avalanche at 9.30 a.m. just as the children were assembling for roll-call. It had been set in motion by springs building up water pressure in the fissured sandstone underlying the tip and when this pressure was released a second wave of liquid mud and sludge roared down and swamped everything below to a depth of 45 feet, including the school playground; 147 people died, mostly from suffocation, 116 of them children.

Men working on the top of the rubbish-mountain, 800 feet high and over 30 years old, saw the waste below them suddenly fall away with a thunderous noise like a black torrential river before it disappeared from view in thick morning fog. Below, a schoolboy saw it uproot a great tree, then swallow up two other boys trying to escape. 'It hit the school like a big wave, spattering all over the place and crushing the buildings. It was like a dream and I was very scared.'

The first rescuers to arrive were miners from two local collieries who had heard the heavy rumble and abandoned their shifts to help. Faint cries were coming from the fringe of the wreckage which was strewn over half a mile and from parts of the school not completely demolished. One of them, knowing his daughter to be there, ran three miles non-stop to reach the building and was seen still digging in the sludge nine hours later. Other men soon joined them, civil defence workers, police, soldiers and a naval detachment of 200 from the cruiser H.M.S. *Tiger* then visiting Cardiff. All day, and by arc-lights on through the night, 2,500 people or more, including mothers and old women scrabbling at the rubbish with their bare hands, toiled frenziedly to reach the victims. The work was slowed at first for lack of heavy earth-moving machinery and until this arrived human chains were formed to carry buckets of sludge. Meanwhile, in the narrow valley traffic problems intensified as more helpers arrived with their equipment impeded by crowds of idle spectators.

An obscene waste of rock, sludge and shale covers the spot where 147 people, most of them children, died in the Pontglas schoolhouse and its neighbouring cottages and farmhouse, when they were engulfed by a 'flow slide' from a nearby coal-tip.

84

This was small consolation for the bereaved, whose grief was mingled with a strong conviction that the disaster could have been averted. The British National Coal Board stated within hours that the cause was recent heavy rainfall. How could that possibly be known? (In fact, the underlying spring was later found to be discharging at the rate of 100,000 gallons an hour.) What about the warnings that many people were said to have uttered over the years? Why had no action been taken? When the official inquest was held to record the cause of the deaths, one distracted father shouted: 'Murdered by the National Coal Board!'

It was in this mood of grief and anger that 10,000 people assembled on 27 October when 81 children were buried in two long communal graves in the hillside cemetery of Aberfan. Above them was laid an immense cross made up of wreaths sent from all over the world, while throughout Britain flags were flown at half-mast on public buildings at the request of Queen Elizabeth. Two days later, on a completely informal visit to the village with Prince Philip, she was visibly moved on being presented with a small posy by a three-year-old girl 'from the surviving children of Aberfan'.

Not only the villagers, but the nation and Parliament were determined that the truth behind this disaster should be uncovered and a Tribunal of Inquiry was set up immediately under Lord Justice Edmund Davies, himself born two miles from Aberfan and with long experience of mining problems. He was given the widest powers to subpoena attendance and call for documents. Meanwhile, pending its conclusions, an immediate check was ordered on 500 other tips in South Wales, and upwards of 200 were found to be in a dangerous condition.

The Tribunal sat in public for 76 days, heard 136 witnesses and published a Report in August 1967, which prompted Lord Robens, Chairman of the Coal Board, to tender his resignation. It was refused.

A key sentence in the Report read: 'Our strong and unanimous view is that the Aberfan disaster could and should have been prevented.' It went on to record 'ignorance on the part of those charged at all levels with

The *Guardian* said: 'It was a day of the most stark and bitter horror . . . The first two bodies found were little girls. They had just entered the rear playground and their hands were still clasped. A teacher was found dead, her body hunched in a corner by a classroom radiator, protecting a group of children huddled under her. But they, too, were dead'. The bodies of 14 more children were found in another classroom and in yet another those of the deputy headmaster, Mr D. Beynon, and five children clasped in his arms.

Terrible as it was, the death-roll affecting 99 families in the village might have been even higher. Many children in the infant classes were saved with their teachers. Mrs Pauline Evans, one of the mothers, rescued children from a classroom facing away from the tip by climbing in through a window. 'When I got inside there were about a dozen children screaming in a room which had only half collapsed. With the help of a nurse I handed them through the window to safety.' Some lucky ones coming by bus from a nearby village had been delayed by the fog and arrived 10 minutes after the tragedy had occurred.

the siting, control and daily management of tips; bungling ineptitude on the part of those who had the duty of supervising and directing them; and failure on the part of those having knowledge of the factors which affect tip safety to communicate that knowledge and see that it was applied.' Many witnesses, even intelligent ones, 'had been oblivious of what lay before their eyes. They were like moles being asked about the habits of birds.'

Blame rested squarely on the National Coal Board and its local officials. Their failure to devise and implement a tipping policy was the basic cause of the disaster. Sound advice and warnings had been ignored. As early as 1927 Professor Knox had drawn attention in a widely publicized paper to the menace to tip stability from uncontrolled water pressure. In 1939, after the partial subsidence of a tip five miles from Aberfan, the then owners, the Powell Duffryn Company, had issued a document underlining the danger and illustrating it with a description of sub-soil conditions exactly applicable to tip 7 (the disaster tip). In 1944, another tip had partially subsided down the mountainside towards Aberfan, providing 'to all who had eyes to see a constant and vivid reminder that tips built on slopes can and do slip and, having once started, can and do travel long distances.'

Late in 1963, there had been a substantial slide of tip 7 itself, strikingly like the final disaster – and still there were no regular inspections or concern shown by the National Coal Board. The slide was not even recorded in its files. 'For nearly three years', said the Report, that event 'presented a vivid warning of the terrible danger which loomed ahead. But it was a warning which no one in authority ever heeded.'

The Tribunal was at pains to refute charges of outright villainy against officials. 'There are no villains in this harrowing story,' said the Report, and a striking simile made this clear. 'Miners devote certainly no more attention to rubbish tips than householders do to dustbins.'

Now all that was to be changed. The Tribunal considered whether mining waste could be disposed of underground, as in some European countries, but this was considered impracticable. Tips would have to continue and were to be left in charge of the Coal Board. In future they were to be treated as potentially dangerous structures subject to regular inspection under the supervision of the Inspectorate of Mines and Quarries. An Advisory Committee on Tip Safety was set up in 1968 with direct responsibility to the Minister for Power and close links with the Secretary for Trade and Industry. Never again were tips to be treated as mere convenient dumps for rubbish.

Certainly this was consoling and every effort was made to help the inhabitants of Aberfan to surmount the tragedy. A disaster fund amounting, when it closed on 31 January 1967, to over £1,600,000 (with donations from 88,000 people) gave a total of £810,000 to 712 villagers, including £5,000 to each of the bereaved families, and further sums for the needs of injured children and the relief of distress in the village. £250,000 and £200,000 were earmarked for the construction and endowment of a magnificent community centre, with a concert hall, swimming pool and play facilities for children, which was opened by the Queen in 1973. Although the remains of tip 7 were declared safe after the fall, in 1968 the Government deferred to the insistence of the inhabitants and its removal was ordered.

Today there is a new school in Aberfan and the children enjoy a safe life. Only the adults are left with their memories, what might have been if, for instance, the warning of Councillor Mrs Gwynneth Williams had been heeded when she spoke, as recorded in the minutes of the Merthyr District Council Planning Committee in January 1964: 'We have had a lot of trouble from slurry causing flooding at Merthyr Vale. If the tip moves it could threaten the whole school.'

Far left : An aerial view of the village of Aberfan shows the ruined school in the centre with rescue workers labouring around it, while in the background the track made by the sludge as it plunged down the hillside can be clearly seen.

Left above : Miners from two neighbouring collieries were among the first of the hundreds of people who came to help. Throughout the day and night rescue workers, including frantic mothers, scrabbled at the sludge. In the narrow valley traffic bringing help was often impeded by idle onlookers.

Far left below : Among the toiling crowds of rescuers, a policeman raises the blanket which covers the pathetic remains of a child.

Left : In the flower bedecked hillside cemetery of Aberfan one of the surviving children mourns beside the simply marked grave of a friend.

Florence, 1966

In the late autumn of 1966 exceptionally severe weather with gales and frequent cloud-bursts struck almost the whole of Europe, raging for several days from Poland across Germany to the shores of the North Sea, down the coast into Holland and across France and Switzerland. In these areas the storms led to some loss of life, considerable damage and great inconvenience. But in Italy they spawned a disaster.

Because of its physical features many parts of Italy have always been subject to heavy flooding. As distinct from Britain, for instance, where the source of most rivers is only slightly above downstream areas, in Italy they rise in many cases thousands of feet above the plains, in the Western Alps, in the Dolomites to the north-east, and in the Apennines, the central ridge which runs like a backbone down the peninsula. In times of heavy rainfall these rivers, reinforced from innumerable mountain streams, pour down at tremendous speed, bringing with them masses of rock and other débris, particularly in the Dolomites where the higher slopes are very unstable. Certain precautions can be taken, of course, dredging river beds, building up banks, but there are times when Nature mocks these efforts.

Such was the case in 1966. Winds rising sometimes to hurricane force swept through the whole length of Italy and brought with them rains of an enormous intensity. It was as though, after weeks of intermittent rain, the sky had suddenly become an ocean which was now falling in a solid mass on the land.

The deluge lasted for two days and in some places, notably the Dolomites, six months' average rainfall came down in 24 hours. This alone would have flooded the northern plains to a depth of several feet, but at least the water would have been fairly stagnant. However, a swirling, destructive tide was created by the rivers swollen yet further by snow melted by warm mountain winds, which burst their banks and roared down at terrifying speed, sweeping aside great stretches of forest that lay in their path and carrying with them an ever-increasing load of rock and débris.

In Friuli-Venezia-Giulia, the north-eastern province at the head of the Adriatic, scores of farms with all their livestock were overwhelmed by floods, avalanches, mud-slides and giant boulders, while in many villages and towns, Trento, for instance, Merano and Bressanone, the streets were submerged in mud to a depth which swallowed up cars and buses. Long sections of road surfaces were completely carried away, railway lines were cut, bridges demolished and so much wreckage was deposited in river-beds that their level in some places rose many feet above roads running alongside.

For a while the north-east provinces were completely cut off except by radio, and an exhausted messenger who reached Venice over mountain tracks from the Dolomites was regarded as a curiosity. He said: 'For days we have been fighting against the fury of rivers without ceasing.'

One third of Italy was stricken by floods which Interior Minister Taviani described as the worst in history. The Po valley was flooded from both ends, by the overflowing river and by salt water when raging seas broke through dykes protecting the delta. Here one third of the population had to be evacuated, including 12,000 from the island of Donzella lying between two branches of the river.

In Venice sea and sky together produced the worst floods in a thousand years, the main danger coming from the sea. The fate of the city still depended on a system of dykes more than 400 years old which linked the islands separating the Lagoon from the Adriatic. Their upkeep had been neglected, especially during World War II, and early in November exceptionally rough seas combined with gales broke through a section of dyke at the island of Pellestrina. Immediately a wall of water poured into the city, rising to a height of seven

Right : The most extensive floods in Italy for more than 25 years raged throughout the north and central parts of the country in November 1966. In Florence, the Arno broke its banks.

Left : Damage done to the shops on the famous Ponte Vecchio shows chaos caused by the flood waters.

feet in some streets and five feet in St Mark's Square, including the cathedral. For 48 hours, until repairs could be carried out and the flood began to subside, life was completely paralyzed.

The London *Times* correspondent reported that Venice was like a gigantic, half-sunken boat. He should have said 'a torpedoed tanker'. Oil storage tanks used for central heating had burst spreading slicks over the flood, and it was this oil-scummed water that ruined the stocks of 4,000 shops, an immense amount of private property and the ground-floor contents of half the city's hotels. Fortunately there was little damage to art treasures. If the gale had continued for only a few more hours, however, the city centre with its magnificent heritage would have been destroyed. Even so, the damage caused was astronomical.

The shops could be restocked, but it would not be so easy to restore agriculture. Before the war, the fertile area of Tuscany known as the Maremma had been largely marshland ridden by malaria. Much of it had been reclaimed and the malaria eradicated, and a thriving industry started based on dairy farming and the production of fruit and vegetables for export. All this was ruined by the floods which submerged four-fifths of the town of Grosetto lying at the centre of the area, 80 per cent of the livestock was destroyed and damage caused exceeded that in the entire province of Venezia.

The heaviest cultural blow was struck at Florence and this aspect of Italy's disaster above all others caught the horrified imagination of the world. Cradle of the Italian Renaissance, a major shrine of western civilization, with its palaces, magnificent Romanesque buildings, and 40 museums housing many of the world's greatest art treasures, Florence was to suffer the fate of Venice – and worse.

On 4 November, the River Arno traversing the oldest part of the city burst its banks. Normally a man running can keep pace with the fastest flowing river, but on this day the Arno in a huge ungovernable flood surged forward at 40 miles an hour (a film made on the spot shows a car being hurled down the Via Formabuoni at just this speed). For several hours the torrent poured through the city spreading ever wider, flooding buildings and rising in places, including the Cathedral Square and the famous eleventh-century Baptistry, to over 15 feet. The best that anyone could do was to save a few possessions and escape drowning. Twenty-four hours later the deluge began to abate, leaving behind a massive residue of glutinous yellow mud, and in the following days it was possible to start surveying the damage. Final estimates showed 17 people dead, 45,000 homeless (a tenth of the population), 40,000 cars wrecked as well as 18,000 shops, including the workshops of some of the goldsmiths and leather-workers for which Florence was famous.

The loss and damage were enormous. Again, oil from burst tanks, and in some places naphtha, mixed with the flood and added to its destructiveness. Many

Above : Cars lie stranded in the waters as soldiers and other rescue workers use a rubber dinghy to paddle stranded Florentines to safety. More than 100,000 people throughout northern Italy were rendered homeless and the final death roll was 112.

Above right : Renaissance palaces and churches suffered severely. The population took to planks to cross the waterlogged streets.

Every job of restoration had to be done as soon as possible to avoid rapid deterioration and speed was achieved by giving crash courses to teams of students and then putting them under the supervision of a single expert. All this caught the attention of the outside world, but naturally the people involved in the 36,000 square miles of Italy that had been devastated were more interested in obtaining credit to get on their feet again. There had been damage in 800 municipalities; 22,000 farms and private homes had suffered; 50,000 animals had been lost, thousands of tractors made useless. Total damage was estimated at £575 million ($1,090 million). The death-roll in all Italy was 112.

In Florence, a fortnight after the disaster, the people were working hard to succour the homeless, start business again and clean up their beautiful city. They were not relying much on government help; they knew official red tape too well. Enthusiasm bursting through his sober prose, the London *Times* correspondent noted: 'Tuscan sturdiness has risen above the ruin of the city's delicate grace.' He noticed an interesting point: it was the 'beatniks', so criticized by their elders as useless drop-outs, who were flinging themselves into relief work with the most astonishing energy. 'Beatniks', he added, 'are better than bureaucrats.'

A year later the people were back in their homes and at work again. Museums, galleries and libraries had re-opened and it was said that: 'The golden city of the Renaissance glitters again.' But despite intensive work on the river-bed and its banks, and the organization of a flood early-warning system, anxiety must remain. Asked what would happen if it rained like *that* again, a city official replied: 'We must just hope that it won't.'

Above: Workers carry the statue of St John the Baptist, by seventeenth-century artist Piemontini, out of the cathedral. It was washed away from its base and decapitated.

Below: The cleaning-up was a massive task, as the mud-strewn square in front of the Church of the Holy Cross indicates.

famous buildings were swamped, among them the Medici Chapel, the San Firenzi Palace, the Casa di Dante, the Capella del Pazzi at Santa Croce and the church of Santa Maria Novella. Six hundred paintings by well-known masters were under water for hours when the basement of the famous Uffizi Gallery was flooded. Totally destroyed at the same time were 130,000 photographic negatives of Florentine art, many of them irreplaceable.

Elsewhere in the city there were other heavy casualties: the entire State Records of Tuscany from the fourteenth century to 1860, nineteenth-century newspaper files – a loss now making a detailed history of the Risorgimento impossible, Etruscan collections in the Archaeological Museum, the musical scores of Scarlatti, the private papers of Amerigo Vespucci (the Italian explorer who gave his name to America) and the earliest painting in Western art, the 'Cruxifixion' by Cimabue (1240–1302).

Worst hit of all were the libraries. For days more than 6,000,000 volumes, a great many of them unique, lay submerged under water and murky sludge in the State Archives and the vaults of the Biblioteca Nazionale, the equivalent of the British Museum Library – a potential loss which would have had a shattering effect on every aspect of future study and research. At once, a massive international rescue operation was set in motion, with experts from all over Europe coming to advise and help. Even so, the restoration, wherever possible, of these works and the paintings was to take years. Owing to the melting of glue used in bindings and size in the paper, many books when salvaged were as solid as bricks. Each volume had to be cleaned, dried, treated with chemicals to prevent fungus and the pages cautiously prised apart. Finally each volume had to be rebound.

Farmington, Virginia, 1968 and Kellogg, Idaho, 1972

'Most coal mines in the United States', said the *New York Times* of 23 November 1968 'are in violation of safety regulations of one kind or another'; and, later, 'The two unavoidably salient facts about the history of coal-mining in the United States are that it has taken an appalling toll of men, and that almost no-one has cared enough to prevent the toll.'

These comments were made after a series of explosions on 20 November 1968, had sparked fierce fires deep below the earth in a soft-coal mine operated by a subsidiary of the Consolidation Coal Company of Pittsburgh. Seventy-eight men died in the disaster in the Consol No. 9 mine, within 10 miles of Monongay, West Virginia, where 361 men had been killed in 1907 in the worst mine disaster in U.S. history. That accident brought into being the U.S. Bureau of Mines, but it was not until 1941 that the Bureau was allowed to send its inspectors on to mine-owners' property except by consent, and by that date more than 12,000 U.S. miners had been killed by underground explosions.

Consol No. 9 mine runs eight miles west and east and six miles north and south, occupying a subterranean coal-seam between the tiny villages of Farmington and Mannington in West Virginia. The mine lies over an oil and natural-gas field. It is in an area where the population has lived from mining for generations and is inured to the possibility of tragedy. When, at 5.40 a.m., an underground explosion shattered the miners' lamp-house where precise records of the men below ground were kept, nobody knew exactly how many were involved. Of the 99 men on the midnight to 8.00 a.m. shift, 21 were known to be safe, but a day of telephone checks to miners' homes finally produced a list of 78 men unaccounted for.

Hours after the initial explosion and the three secondary blasts that followed it, dense black smoke from the fire still rose in a column several hundred feet high over the blasted Llewellyn portal, one of the entrances to the mine, near Manningtree, from which the miners had descended to a depth of 600 feet at midnight.

Rescue attempts had to be put off for fear of further explosions, as teams waited by the mine's nine portals. During the day workmen placed brick-and-concrete seals over two of the ventilation shafts, to try to direct the air flow away from the fire and contain it in one area, thus giving the men a chance to escape to another part of the mine; but at 10.00 p.m. on the night after the first explosion, another blast – apparently of methane gas deep in the mine – blew out the seals, and flames again roared from the wrecked portals, causing a glow in the night sky which apparently could be seen for many miles around.

At the rescue headquarters news of the latest explosion was regarded as a bad sign. Officials began speaking of days and even weeks before conditions would allow rescue teams to enter the blazing mine.

The only hope was that the trapped men had been able to escape into an area remote from that of the explosion – the area from which the 21 men who had escaped the disaster had been rescued or had left after feeling the concussion. But the rescuers were pessimistic. Only two ventilation fans were still working to provide air to the sections of the mine not yet touched by the fire, and it was doubtful if the men could have reached them,

Huge clouds of smoke pour from the Llewellyn Portal of the soft coal mine near Farmington, Virginia, Of the 99 men trapped only 21 escaped.

even using the breathing apparatus kept in lockers in the mine, which could keep a man alive for several days.

As the days passed hopes dwindled. The fire still raged and relations, stoically waiting for news, were kept away from the mine for fear of further explosions. They were kept informed of events by loudspeaker as work continued in the attempt to divert the course of the fire. But another explosion indicated that it had turned west and gone back to the area where the men were believed to be trapped, and fire and smoke belched anew from the main shaft.

The rescue work was almost impossible. The trapped miners would have had about an hour to find a sanctuary from the fire and barricade it with rock, but nobody really thought they could have survived the blast, the heat, and the gas. The only way to stop the fire was to starve it of air, but this would also mean the end of all hope for the men. Ventilation holes were drilled from the surface to the mine galleries in which the men were most likely to be, and a measuring device lowered, but no contact was made.

Further explosions and the appearance of smoke at the Mahan portal, south-west of Manningtree, showed that the fire had swept through the mine corridors into one of the two underground areas where last-ditch rescue efforts were being concentrated. Boreholes were drilled to sample the air in these areas, and the test showed that it was high in methane, low in oxygen and showed some signs of carbon-monoxide. Asked if this could support life, Consol's executive vice president said, after a long pause, 'It is possible'.

This reply was the end of hope for the waiting relations, and on 30 November the mine was finally sealed. 'Cumulative evidence,' the court said as it granted permission, 'shows without question that life is not possible where the men would be located'.

At once the recrimination started. The explosion had undoubtedly been caused by the igniting of the methane gas which was liberated from the coal seam at the rate of eight cubic feet every 24 hours. Consol said the mine was only moderately gassy and that the gas was diluted by the ventilation network. The Bureau said it was extremely gassy. But the tragic fact was that the mine proved to be unsafe.

*   *   *   *

A gas – carbon-monoxide in this case – and a 'callous disregard for safety' also caused the deaths of 91 men in a silver mine in the rugged hills of North Idaho in May 1972. The mine, six miles east of Kellogg with its population of 7,000, is one of the richest and deepest silver mines in the United States, and it has rambled through so much ground that it is now like 'a big apartment house with many rooms'.

The fire which broke out on the morning of 2 May in a worked-out portion of the mine, 3,700 feet underground, was probably caused by spontaneous combustion of old timbers supporting the shafts, where temperatures often exceed 100°F. Smoke from the burning timbers entered the mine's main ventilation-shafts and spread quickly. All day the ominous trail of white smoke which billowed from the mine's exhaust stack indicated that the fire still burned underground, and fresh air was pumped in feverishly. Teams wearing oxygen masks groped through tunnels, sealing off

A week after a silver mine in North Idaho caught fire, two young miners were found alive and well, 4,800 feet below ground. Tom Wilkenson, pictured above climbing from the rescue capsule, and Tom Flory were the only two to survive among 93 men trapped in the mine who suffocated. when smoke from the burning timbers entered the main ventilation shafts.

empty shafts and searching for men. Although a number of men were brought out, 24 bodies were found and the only hope of reaching further survivors was to penetrate to the lower levels of the mine where men might have fled through some of the hundred miles of tunnels to safety.

While rescuers worked on, now using a capsule, lowered through a narrow shaft at the end of a half-inch steel cable, to take rescue workers down the mine, the inquiry into the disaster had already started. In this area, known as Silver Valley, mining is a way of life. Although the men know the risks of the job – sometimes the mines are so hot that they can only work for half an hour – the rewards are so great that they stay on. Safety training, said some of the men, was non-existent. Survivors did not know how to use the respirators which were provided; and when the elevator operators died through the lack of self-rescue chemical-masks the elevators stopped running, since it was impossible to operate them from above ground.

A week after the fire began searchers found two men 4,800 feet down, and in good health. They said that they and seven others had led the race for safety down the horizontal drift, or shaft, towards a lower level. One of the two men stumbled; the other dragged him into the fresh air of a lower tunnel and went back to look for the others, but all were dead, overcome by smoke and carbon monoxide gas. For a week the two men waited, making their way to the lower levels where they had been told to go in the event of a fire because fresh air would be piped into the shaft. There they had waited. The lights on their hats burnt out, but they were sustained by the food and drink taken from the lunch buckets of the men who had died.

Relatives rushed to the mine with renewed hope, but by now 47 bodies had been found, and hopes for the missing men suffered another blow when a massive cave-in severed lines carrying compressed air. Eventually, on 10 May, the last of the 91 bodies was found and brought out. This had been the largest metal-mine disaster since fire in a mine in 1917 released carbon-monoxide gas which, through lack of breathing apparatus and a shortage of escape aids, killed 163 men in Butte, Montana.

Peru, 1970

In those parts of the world which, through faults in the earth's crust, are particularly susceptible to earthquakes, the people learn to live with the risk and to accept it as part of their lives, in the same way that people who live in the northern hemisphere accept the probability of snow in winter.

Peruvians have been aware of the likelihood of earthquakes throughout the centuries (the recorded history of earthquakes in Peru dates back to the Spanish chroniclers of 1619) and have learned to accept them philosophically. Few, however, imagined such a devastating earthquake as the one which occurred on Sunday, 1 May 1970, affecting 600 miles of the Peruvian coast and a vast hinterland, leaving dozens of towns in ruins or totally obliterated, and killing a staggering total of at least 50,000 people.

Peruvians are ardent football fans, and at 3.00 that afternoon most of them had settled down at home to watch the first match of the World Cup series on television. Twenty-three minutes later, out at sea, 50 miles west of the thriving fishing town of Chimbote with its population of 200,000, the ocean bed cracked and heaved. The earth, tortured by stress, sought to find for itself a more comfortable position, like an old man turning in bed; and all along a 250-mile stretch of coastline, bounded by Trujillo in the north and Lima, the capital, in the south, the ground heaved and shook in a mighty earthquake which achieved an intensity of between seven and eight degrees on the Richter scale. For many hundreds of miles north, south and east across the land, the shock was felt.

At first the magnitude of the disaster was not appreciated. In Lima, people rushed into the streets, but the capital was fortunate and escaped without damage. Not for some hours, for all communications had been cut, was it learned that the full force of this 'act of God' had

Below : Roads winding over the hillsides disappear into the sea of mud and snow, caused by a vast landslide from Mount Huascarán, which has completely engulfed the town of Yungay and most of its 25,000 inhabitants. Only the tips of palm trees can be seen where they once stood in the main square, the Plaza de Armas.

Yungay was here

Plaza de Armas
(main square)

been felt by Chimbote, which lay on the narrow coastal plain, and by the towns and villages inland, in the foothills of the Andean mountain range.

Early reports, even then, seriously underestimated the magnitude of the disaster. They spoke of '250 killed in Chimbote' and '140 in Huaraz'. Slowly the shocking truth emerged: Chimbote lay in ruins and an estimated 2,700 people had died. Casma, Huanmey and all the towns along the coast had suffered to a greater or lesser extent, and unknown thousands of people had been killed. It was quite impossible to discover what had happened inland, in the district of Callejon de Huaylas, a popular tourist area known as the 'Switzerland of Peru', where lay hundreds of mountain towns and small villages.

Radio communication was silenced as a result of damage to the hydro-electric station at Huallanca; roads were impassable through landslides and subsidence; and when, next day, helicopters attempted to reconnoitre, the pilots' view was obscured by mist and huge clouds of dust rising thousands of feet into the air. Nobody knew what had happened in an area the size of Scotland, dominated by the 22,205-foot-high peak of Mount Huascaran.

An hour after the earthquake it was already apparent that the magnitude of the disaster was far greater than the authorities in Lima had originally imagined. The President of Peru, General Velasco, set sail in a naval vessel for Chimbote (for the coastal roads were blocked by landslides, the airfields were unusable and there was always the fear of further tremors) with various senior officials. The next morning he inspected the ruined town and neighbouring Casma and Coishco, and visited the injured at an emergency hospital. Before he returned to Lima – bringing some of the injured on the ship with him – in order to direct rescue operations, he attempted to visit the mountainous Callejón de Huaylas, but it was still impossible.

At Chimbote, General Velasco had found a town in ruins; 60–70 per cent of the buildings were destroyed, the old part of the town, where many buildings were in poor condition, being the worst affected. Almost nothing, whether concrete or adobe, had escaped damage. Despite the efforts of the rescue parties, dozens of people still lay under the rubble, injured and perhaps dying. Many hundreds more camped in the street; some had no roof beneath which to shelter, others were afraid of further earth tremors.

From the Callejón de Huaylas, isolated behind rock-barred roads, confused and unconfirmed reports suggested even worse destruction. Aircraft were still hampered by bad visibility and vast dust-clouds. Eventually an amateur radio operator from within the mountain fastnesses managed to make contact and, with his plea 'Don't forget us!', the world first learned that the town of Yungay and a part of nearby Ranrahirca had completely disappeared under a landslide from Huascaran. Later, the Air Force confirmed this news: a vast wall of mud and snow had swept down the mountainside and, divided by a spur of hills, swallowed the two small towns.

Of Yungay, where the few survivors had managed to flee to the cemetery on the edge of the town, all that could be seen were the tips of the 100-foot-high palm-trees which had stood in the main square. A helicopter

pilot reported that he had counted a dozen more towns, each of between two and three thousand inhabitants, which were now merely heaps of stones.

For two and a half days no helicopter was able to land in the Andes region because of the continuing bad visibility. Until a hundred parachutists managed to land, the only contact with these isolated regions came from the desperate, pleading voice of the radio amateur.

The very size of the area of devastation meant that much of it was inaccessible, and it was many days before relief-workers – their resources stretched to the utmost – managed to reach remoter parts. One of the problems was to know just what supplies were needed. In the mountain villages hundreds of thousands of Indian peasants remained without heating, food or shelter for almost a week. Throughout the area survivors poured on to the passable roads on foot, in carts and lorries, desperately seeking help and refuge. Distracted people made for their nearest towns – often to find, like the two injured village policemen who staggered into Huaraz three days after the earthquake, that the hoped-for sources of assistance were themselves in desperate straits. Without the much-needed help the death-toll mounted steeply.

On the coastal plain rescue operations continued, and relief-workers and aid of all kinds poured in from all over the world. So great was the task in this region, scattered with huge *haciendas* farming sugar or maize, that in Chimbote, despite the all-pervading smell of fish-meal from the damaged factory, five days after the

Above : As rescue workers managed to reach the victims of the villages and towns situated away from the coast, they were taken to the nearest centres for help. This plane-load of victims is being flown from the Huaylas area to the seaside town of Chimbote.

Below : In Lima, some distance from the epicentre of the shock wave, startled and terrified spectators at the Monterrice Hippodrome run out on to the track as they feel the first tremors of the earthquake which was to kill so many of their countrymen.

earthquake rescue workers could still use their noses to find more and more dead bodies under the rubble. And still the number of dead and dying in the mountain villages in a region some 300 miles long and 120 miles wide could only be guessed at.

The fear continued. From time to time small earth tremors could be felt and when, a couple of days after the earthquake, the ground again trembled, people rushed into the streets in their night-clothes, their hands sheltering their heads. Many preferred to sleep in the open; and the new 'houses', built on the rubble of the old, were made of harmless rushes. Some feared even to sleep, for they had heard that the mountain lakes could break their natural barriers, causing disastrous floods.

This particular horror, however, was spared the luckless population. Although many valley streams turned into torrents, there was comparatively little damage from water; nor did a tidal-wave follow upon the earthquake, the ocean level varying only by a few feet from its normal level.

Rock falls and avalanches, however, had caused major damage. Of these, the greatest and most catastrophic was that which destroyed Yungay and Ranrahirca and killed nearly 30,000 people in these and in neighbouring small towns and villages. On that day, 5,000 feet up in the heights of Huascaran, a party of Japanese mountain climbers visiting this famous mountain resort found themselves the horrified but fascinated spectators of this event. The avalanche began with an almost vertical fall of 10,000 feet of a vast mass of ice and rock, almost a third of a mile wide and nearly two miles long, from the western face of Mount Huascaran. Impelled by the two-mile height of its initial fall, this gigantic mass then poured down the valley at a speed estimated at nearly 250 miles an hour. The million cubic yards of ice that had become detached from the highest point of the glacier then set another 24 million cubic yards in motion.

In the path of this unimaginable terror lay small villages and the towns of Yungay on the west and Ranrahirca on the east of a mountain spur. Above Yungay, a 600-foot hill was swept up in the path of the avalanche and deposited on the other side of the valley. This and the unfortunate mountain towns absorbed the force of the huge landslide. Other rock- and earth-falls blocked roads, particularly in the coastal areas

where the road-side slopes were steep, dammed the River Santa at Recuhat, and destroyed countless houses. Many of these slides took place in stages, giving the threatened population time to flee: but in Yungay and Ranrahirca there was small hope of escaping the roaring death . . . and only eight years after Ranrahirca and seven mountain villages had been the previous victims of the Nevado de Huascaran's monstrous ice-cap, when a part of it broke loose killing 3,000 people.

It took many weeks for the people of the devastated regions to recover from the effects of 'the giant's hand', as one Indian peasant called it, and the villages in the steep Andean valleys, tucked under the towering cliffs, suffered most severely through their sheer inaccessibility. Freezing rain made it even more difficult for troops and parachutists to reach the population, and thus nearly as many died from the aftermath of the earthquake as during the event itself.

In the valleys life came back to normal more quickly. The 'uncomprehending silence', which one observer reported as brooding over shattered towns, turned to the noise and bustle of people trying to rebuild shattered lives. And when, on 2 June, Peru beat Bulgaria in a World Cup match, people even found the heart to cheer, and red-and-white Peruvian flags were planted to wave proudly over pathetic heaps of rubble that had once been homes.

Thousands of people without homes tried to organize new lives – and many realized they would be homeless for a long time. For many, too, there were no more jobs. Young people with knapsacks took to the roads, making for the sugar capital in the north, Trujillo. 'What is the point', one asked 'of rebuilding here?' And indeed with the trade of the towns disrupted and with little, poorly paid, work available on the *haciendas*, their reactions were reasonable. Once again it was the mountain peasants, who knew no other way of life, who suffered most harshly.

It seemed that the whole of Peru and half the world were anxious to help in the vast task of rehabilitation. Peruvian authorities encouraged visits from journalists and notable foreigners who would tell the rest of the world what had happened, and thus recruit much needed aid of all kinds.

Where any disaster is concerned the question that is always asked afterwards is: 'What could have been done to prevent it?' Where natural events are concerned, particularly in the case of one so overwhelming as the Peruvian earthquake, the answer must be 'Very little'. Most of man's protection must lie in warnings which are the result of constant vigilance. Hurricane, flood and avalanche warnings are now commonplace in many parts of the world; and even if they are sometimes too late, they help to save many lives. Predicting an earthquake is more difficult, but the steady series of major disasters to which the world is prone makes it apparent that research into both the prevention and warning of earthquakes is of vital importance.

The imminence of an earthquake can sometimes be detected by continuous monitoring of the fluctuations of the earth's magnetic field, its seismic activities and the strain and tilt of the earth's crust. Just as a threatened ice-fall can be safely triggered off, under controlled conditions, by the use of explosives, so explosives and drilling techniques could be used to provoke land movement and unlock dangerous faults under strain. So far, however, this is a science which has made few practical advances and 'the giant's hand' continues to crush and maim throughout the world.

Many lessons were learned from Peru's disaster. It became apparent that destruction would have been less if buildings had been better sited or better constructed. In the area affected by the worst of the earthquake, the damage was caused mainly to buildings which were of poor quality, unsuited to the type of soil on which they were constructed, and erected on badly laid foundations. The earthquake opened cracks in the saturated sand and clay soils and increased the level of underground water; while rock-sited foundations were not so seriously affected. In Huaraz, for example, the older part of the town, built on the alluvium of the river, suffered the greatest damage; the new part, however, built on rock brought down by a landslide in 1941, was less damaged. Mud-brick buildings proved to be less equal to strain than brick or concrete, but in some cases concrete buildings collapsed because of the poor materials used in their construction.

These lessons are learnt at a fearful cost. In the final analysis, man's puny efforts are all useless when Nature decides to unleash the full fury of her powers.

From all over the world help was rushed to Peru. Although for many days it was impossible to reach some of the mountain villages, made inaccessible by reason of weather or impassable roads, the rescuers struggled on through conditions which were sometimes hazardous in the extreme.

Below: Eventually even the most remote villages were reached, supplies of all kinds were brought in and homeless people were helped to erect tents and provide themselves with temporary shelters.

The Club Cinq-Sept, 1970

Big fires involving heavy loss of life are inevitably followed by official inquiries, accusations of crir nal neglect, recriminations, sackings and promises of immediate reforms so that disaster cannot happen again – until it does happen again, somewhere else.

Absolute security against fire is almost impossible to create. Fire-prevention literature outlines three basic factors on which the outbreak of fire depends, known as the 'fire triangle': the presence of fuel, sufficient heat to ignite the fuel and enough oxygen to support combustion. The protection of life and property from fire is said to depend on the limitation as far as possible of combustible fuels, the sub-division of buildings into areas small enough to be controllable and building designs which enable people to be quickly and safely evacuated.

The facts of everyday life are different. The presence of 'combustible fuels' is universal and 'sufficient heat' can be represented by a single cigarette-end or burning match. The mere idea of safe evacuation from some buildings must raise a hollow laugh. The danger of disastrous fire remains widespread especially when coupled with the tendency to neglect possibilities thought to be remote.

It was no more than this which led to the deaths of 146 young people (142 immediately, four later in hospital) in a club near the little town of St Laurent du Pont, France, on Saturday, 1 November 1970. The club was called the Cinq-Sept and had only been open a few months. It was housed inside a large shed cheaply built of breeze-blocks with a corrugated iron roof, an arrangement which positively invited disaster. At ground level there was a dance-floor and beyond it a restaurant with bar. Pillars supporting the roof were wound with flimsy coloured materials and around the floor were simulated grottos with archways, walls and ceilings made of plastic (expanded polyurethane). Above, a gallery reached by a single spiral staircase ran right round the building and this, too, was divided into cosy alcoves constructed in the same manner.

The young people present on that night came from all over the region, from Grenoble, 20 miles away, from Aix-les-Bains and Chambery especially to hear an up-and-coming pop group from Paris called 'Storm'. For a club of its size, French fire regulations stipulated three access doors and two emergency exits. On that night the only way to get in or out was by the main entrance controlled by a spiked turnstile too high to be vaulted. A second entrance had been blocked up during building operations and the third had been locked to prevent gate-crashers. Neither exit was illuminated; one was hidden behind a screen near the bandstand, the other had chairs in front of it. Both were locked and the keys were held separately by two of the three managers.

Around 1.40 a.m., in the hilarity backed by the rhythmic pounding of 'Storm', a careless youth in one of the upper alcoves dropped a lighted match on a cushion stuffed with plastic foam. The cover caught fire and melted the foam which gave off toxic fumes. The youngster and friends tried to beat out the fire, but had to stagger back. Before they could breathe freely again, flames were roaring up out of control. Said one survivor later: 'People in the gallery were enveloped by flames. The whole ceiling seemed to catch light. It all happened so quickly. Everything was just one blazing mass.'

There was a surge for the spiral staircase. Thirty people managed to escape through the turnstile. Among the last to get out was Mlle Joelle Dandry, the cashier. A big fire can create a freak turbulence of extraordinary power. Now, from the gallery, 'a huge flame leaped into the air and suddenly plunged to the main floor like a whirlwind. I tried to save myself,' said the cashier. 'Suddenly I felt my hair burning. Everybody was screaming. Then I could hear nothing except the sirens of the fire-engines arriving. I'm sure I was the last person to leave that unimaginable hell alive.'

M. Gilbert Bas, 25, the only surviving manager, was in his office when a flashing alarm told him there was trouble. 'I thought that, as sometimes happens in an establishment like ours, it was simply a fight.' Then he heard screams of 'Fire!', ran to the dance-floor and saw 'the huge sheet of flame. It burned all of them in a matter of seconds. Those that got out after the big burst were walking torches.'

The whole building was a cauldron of flame and highly toxic smoke from the melting plastic. One

Below: A crowd of young people sit listening as a pop group plays at the Club Cinq-Sept. This picture was taken just a week before the tragic fire which killed 146 boys and girls, who must have been sitting in just such a way listening to the up-and-coming group from Paris called the 'Storm', in what were to be the last few minutes of their lives.

barman wrenched aside the chairs blocking an emergency exit and with a few others battered his way out through the door. A youth with particularly quick reactions who had escaped through the turnstile with his girl friend came back round the outside, heard a girl screaming behind one of the locked doors, broke through it and released her. Behind her he saw a mass of people with groping, outstretched arms, already dead. 'If the emergency exits had not been closed', he told reporters, 'very many people would have got out alive.'

Meanwhile, another serious deficiency had taken its toll. Extraordinary for a club isolated by a mile from all other buildings, there was no telephone at the Cinq-Sept, and Gilbert Bas had to waste precious minutes driving into St Laurent to raise the alarm. When the firemen finally arrived their first sight as they ran to break in was the body of a boy impaled on the spikes of the turnstile. The corrugated roof had melted in the heat and inside were 142 charred corpses. Some couples were found on the floor in each other's arms, some were still sitting along the walls where they had been overwhelmed. According to doctors who examined them later, many had died of asphyxiation before the flames reached them. 'It was a terrible sight', said one fireman. 'They didn't have a chance. The place went up like a matchbox.'

It was some hours before the work of removing the dead could begin. With the daylight, groups of young people, many of them friends of the victims, gathered to watch in stunned silence as ambulances transferred stretchers with anonymous burdens to the town hall, now serving as a mortuary. For them it was an act of respect; not so for those that are always drawn to disasters, who now poured in, jamming the roads from St Laurent until a force of 200 men was brought in to control them.

In the morning all shops were closed and the streets of the town were shuttered as relatives waited with dull foreboding by the town hall to identify personal posses-

Above : The simulated grottoes made of expanded polyurethane, and the flimsy materials twined round pillars were largely blamed for the total destruction caused by the fire. Highly inflammable, they helped to reduce the Club Cinq-Sept to this twisted shell within minutes.

Below : Rows of coffins were laid out in the town hall of St Laurent du Pont. Here a short ecumenical service was held amid terrible scenes of grief.

sions carefully collected in envelopes marked only with the sex of the person concerned – jewellery, key-rings, bits of charred clothing. Most of the bodies had been burned beyond recognition.

Next day, rows of coffins were laid out in the town hall among a mountain of flowers which included wreaths from President Pompidou, M. Chaban Delmas the Prime Minister, and foreign governments. Then, in a room too small to hold all the mourners, a short ecumenical service was held amid terrible scenes of grief.

On Tuesday, 4 November, the Mayor and the Secretary-General of the *Département de L'Isère* were relieved of their duties by the French Cabinet. Eight months later, in June 1971, the Mayor and three building contractors were convicted of causing injury through negligence and given short suspended sentences. Gilbert Bas, manager of the club, received a two-year suspended sentence for manslaughter.

An official inquiry set up in Grenoble revealed a series of omissions and evasions extending to every department of the local administration responsible for enforcing national building and safety regulations, some of which had become law as recently as 1969. Planning permission had been given for the construction of the club, but the finished structure had not been inspected by the Building Safety and Fire Departments, as the law required. Regulations regarding exits, internal fire-fighting equipment (totally absent at the Cinq-Sept) and the incorrect materials used in decoration had not been noticed, and the club had opened without permission from the Mayor. It was said that the Police Chief of Grenoble and other high officials had been guests at the club only three days before the fire, and nothing amiss had been noticed.

In France, nearly 30 years later, an almost identical chain of cause and effect, official negligence and private indifference had led to the same sickening disaster as at the Cocoanut Grove in Boston – even down to the probable cause, a lighted match.

The Joelma Building, 1974

São Paulo is Brazil's largest city. Every 24 hours, on average, the population of 8,000,000 is swollen by 1,000 new arrivals from all over the country, 60 new buildings are completed and room has to be found for 300 more cars, the property of residents. It has the phenomenal expansion rate of five per cent a year and already produces nearly 60 per cent of Brazil's industrial wealth. With as many skyscrapers as there are quills on a porcupine, São Paulo, it has been said, is constantly dismantling and rebuilding itself. Construction never ceases, road-drills are never silent and there is so much dust that the inhabitants say it is the only city on earth where it is quite possible actually to see the air you breathe.

At the best of times, São Paulo is a noisy and somewhat dangerous place to live in, with high infant mortality, a high rate of crime, bursting with the ruthless and often anti-social energies of first-generation city-dwellers on the make.

But on the morning of 1 February 1974, something else was added. Pandemonium gripped the city when it was realized that one of its newest office blocks, the 25-storey Joelma Building was ablaze. The first six floors of this building were taken up by a car park. Above that were the offices of the Crefisul Bank and on the upper floors were more offices. In all there were about 650 people in the Joelma when fire broke out on the 11th floor (perhaps in an over-heated air-conditioning vent) and spread upwards through the building with terrifying lightning speed.

About 300 who were below the seat of the fire escaped without difficulty into the street, but within minutes the remainder were trapped. In that time 70 or so braved the flames already engulfing them and stampeded down the stairs, but only a few reached safety. A porter on the tenth floor saw them come, before he, too, made a dash for freedom. 'Men were tearing off their ties and shirts', he said later. 'I saw women stripping off their clothing and everybody was shoving like mad to get down. When someone fell, the mob trampled over him; I saw a young girl trampled to death. On the eleventh floor I saw people run through a barrier of fire with their hair and clothing in flames. Others just stood there petrified and did not move until the flames swallowed them up.'

As firemen arrived with ladders too short and hoses not powerful enough to reach the upper storeys, it soon became only too clear that the city authorities had not given proper thought to the intricate problem of fire precautions in tall buildings. As the Fire Chief, Colonel Ribeiro, said later – after being sacked as a scapegoat – they had quite simply shown lack of interest.

The result now was that the fire could not be contained, and those still alive in the building had only two choices: to jump to death from the windows or scramble up on to the flat roof. Even there the heat and smoke

were intense and people could be seen running helplessly to and fro with outstretched arms, crying out for rescue, but for a long time rescue was impossible. For two hours a bunch of helicopters hovered overhead, unable to land; when the pilots tried to, the paint peeled off the doors and there was an imminent risk of the petrol tanks exploding. All they could do was to drop cartons of milk, to ease throats and lungs scorched by the fumes, and lower ropes which in desperation some people tried to climb, mostly to fall to their deaths. Eventually, when the fire had abated, the planes were able to touch down and a little band of blackened half-crazed survivors was picked up, perhaps as many as 80 of them in all.

Meanwhile, the flames raged on unchecked. Incredibly, live television coverage had been allowed by the authorities and a densely-packed throng of sightseers had been drawn to the scene from a wide area, blocking approach roads with their abandoned cars and causing serious problems for the rescue services. Hypnotized, they watched as people flung themselves from upper windows to escape the flames or clung to ledges till their strength gave out and they heard one man scream 'Goodbye, goodbye . . .' as he fell.

Above and right: The Joelma building in São Paulo was one of many skyscrapers in that grandiose modern city. But when the building caught fire, the ladders and hoses of the fire-fighting appliances proved to be woefully inadequate, and 227 people were suffocated or burnt to death, or died in a frantic attempt to leap to safety.

Intrepid rescuers with equipment like harpoon-guns fired ropes from nearby buildings, then crawled across to ferry individuals, pick-a-back, one at a time to safety. One fireman, José Rufino, saved 18 people in this way, then, half across with the nineteenth, collided with a man falling from a higher floor. The passenger was wrenched from his back, but Rufino carried on, and survived.

Outside, at street level, where onlookers jostled for a better view, firemen held up a large placard: 'Courage, we are with you.' But the words were almost meaningless, though no doubt the men were just as horrified at their inability to help as the priest, found later in tears, who said: 'I was not able to get there in time to give the last rites to any of them.'

It took four hours to get the fire under control, by which time the upper floors were a sodden, twisted shambles and the death-toll had mounted to 227, many of the bodies being reduced to ashes in temperatures estimated to have reached 700° Centigrade.

There was an inquiry amid a spate of stories suggesting sabotage. A telephonist at the Crefisul Bank said she had received an anonymous call about a bomb that had been planted (then why had she not reported it?). Firemen found a badly charred drum of paint-thinning fluid on the 11th floor near the spot where the fire had probably started.

More important than such conjectures were lessons for the future in a city cluttered with similar tall buildings. The first and most obvious deficiency was the provision of only 13 fire-stations with a total of 1,300 men to serve a population of 8,000,000. This was a serious matter, especially in the context of safety over the whole city area. Would ten times the number of stations and men have coped any better with the Joelma fire? It seems unlikely. Fires in skyscrapers must be contained from inside rather than extinguished from outside, and in their failure to plan for this possibility it was the city authorities who were to blame.

The Mayor, Miguel Colasuonno, who was an engineer by trade, put his finger on the trouble when he said that the fire had spread rapidly through the upper floors because large amounts of inflammable plastic had been used in interior paintwork and flooring, and that new regulations to deal with the problem of fire in high-rise buildings must come into force as soon as possible. These should have included the compulsory installation of fire-proof floors in skyscrapers, the use of non-combustible materials throughout interiors and the provision of specially-insulated emergency stairways.

*　　*　　*　　*

All this was standard practice in the U.S.A. where what might have been a terrible disaster was averted on Saturday, 28 July 1945, just because of such precautions. On the morning of that day a B-25 Mitchell bomber weighing 10 tons crashed in dense fog into the Empire State Building between the 78th and 79th floors (24 floors below the top), battering a hole 18 feet by 20. One engine went crashing like a thunderbolt through the entire building; the other fell down a lift shaft. Then the petrol tanks exploded with a roar, throwing up a spear of flame 100 feet high and showering the outer walls with blazing petrol. Inside, more petrol set

the 79th floor ablaze. But even there, where the danger was greatest, of 20 women attending a Catholic Welfare Conference 11 were able to escape down the fire-proof emergency stairs. Again, on the 80th and 86th floors, where 60 sightseers were enjoying the view from an observation lounge, the same story was repeated and nearly everyone escaped, panic being avoided because the stairs, spelling safety, were known to exist.

The experience of two men on the 80th floor was typical: 'We were lifted three feet out of our chairs', said one, 'and thrown on to the floor. I thought it was a Japanese bomb.' With a girl lift operator who had been badly burned, they first tried to reach the stairs by a corridor and when they found it full of flames they hacked their way through a thin office wall to another corridor leading to the stair-head.

The fires in the whole building were got under control comparatively quickly and only 14 people lost their lives. Luckily, it was a Saturday and the Empire State, which normally houses 25,000, held only a few hundred. But if it had been like the Joelma with no proper escape system, there is no doubt that the result would have been very different.

In São Paulo fire precautions had been badly neglected with, as emerged after the disaster, almost criminal folly. The neglect was highlighted by the Director of the Police Technical Department when he revealed that his laboratories were not even capable of testing and developing fire-proof materials: help would have to be sought from abroad. The last word was spoken by a highly-placed Brazilian architect who agreed with what the Fire Chief had said about official lack of interest and added that this was due to the character of his countrymen. According to him, they were always happy to draw up grandiose plans, which they did very well, and the proof of this was São Paulo itself with its motorways stacked ingeniously one above the other, and the fantastic conglomerate of sky-scrapers. When it came to details such as fire precautions, they were not so interested; these, they tended to think, would look after themselves.

For Brazilians, *The Towering Inferno* is a vivid portrayal of the results of such negligence. The film follows only too closely the tragedy in São Paulo.

Within minutes after the start of the fire the only way out was via the roof where there was a helicopter landing stage. But it was two hours before the heat had abated sufficiently for the machines to land and only 80 people, half-crazed with heat, were rescued.

Turkish DC10, Ermenonville Forest, 1974

Flags of 18 nations, topped with black crepe, fluttered over the scene. A thousand people, many still suffering the shock of their bereavement two months earlier, stood in silence. They were only a tiny fraction of those who had wanted to be there, at Thiais, near Orly airport. The others could only mourn in their native lands, hundreds, thousands, of miles away.

Few could understand more than a small part of the ceremony. It was opened in English by the Vicar of the Anglican Church in Paris. After him came Catholics, Jews, priests of the Armenian Christian Church, Mullahs from Turkey, Morocco and Pakistan, Buddhist priests from Japan, and a holy man from India.

Perhaps the words of M. Achille-Fould, French Aviation Minister, were the most moving: 'The worldwide family of all in aviation is in mourning. May the earth of France lie easily on those we commit to it. France, too, looks on them as her own children.' It was France's epitaph on history's greatest air disaster.

Though a few bodies had been identified and handed over to relatives for burial, most of the staggering, tragic, total of 346 instantly killed men, women and children were being committed to a foreign grave on this spring Thursday of 1974 – 9 May. The actual burial would not be public; that would take place in a few days' time, using heavy earth-moving machinery.

The worst air disaster in history had taken almost twice as many lives as any single accident before. At the time of writing, it still holds that unenviable record. It was what every airline had dreaded: an accident to a fully loaded, wide-body jet. As the mystery unfolded, grief gave way to bitterness. It *need* not have happened; it *should* not have happened. Who was to blame?

The DC10 of Turkish Airlines had flown in from Turkey and made a perfect landing at Orly Airport near Paris. Weather conditions were good on that early spring Sunday morning, 3 March, and the pilot taxied briskly up to the terminal buildings; almost immediately passengers started to embark and fill up his lightly-loaded aircraft, while those who had just landed were asked to stay on board. According to airline officials, 216 adult passengers and one infant embarked at Orly.

The need to get more than 200 people on a flight for which they had not booked meant that documentation was hasty. It seemed over the next harrowing hours, that not all of the passengers had been listed; at least one man was travelling on a passport not his own, and some were using other people's tickets.

The plane re-started its three giant General Electric jets, and taxied along to the take-off runway at a few minutes past noon, carrying 335 passengers and 11 crew. In two minutes the DC10 was off, climbing powerfully into the bright sunny sky of France, the three engines – one under each wing, a third in the tail – belching vapour and exhaust. The time: 12.30 p.m.

The plane climbed fast on a wide eastern sweep to skirt Paris. Flight plans ordained that when eventually it turned to its north-west course for London it would be at 16,000 feet. Controllers of France's Northern Air Region watched it on their radar screens as it reached a height of 13,000 feet.

And then, quite simply, the plane vanished from all screens.

At 12.35 it crashed into a shallow depression within the Ermenonville State Forest north-east of Paris.

On that warm Sunday there were many people strolling along the numerous wooded pathways, but although the huge aircraft ploughed a thousand-yard furrow through the trees, shearing them off before kinetic energy was expanded and the wreckage had come to rest, no-one on the ground was hurt.

It had happened without any warning. Some claimed to have seen the aircraft explode in the sky; others had seen it under apparently perfect control, seeming to make an approach towards some not-too-distant airfield. Others, more expert, had seen it in difficulties at a low altitude, trying to drag its nose up from a shallow dive.

Thirty-five minutes after the crash, rescuers arrived by helicopter. One glance showed their journey had been in vain. Little fires, like those of an Indian village, were separated by hundreds of yards, indicating where parts of the engines and fuel system had ended. Bits of fuselage and the débris of human possessions were strewn over the ground; tatters of clothing festooned the branches of trees which had escaped destruction. No one could have survived for an instant.

Meanwhile, at London's Heathrow Airport, there was alarm as the DC10 became first late, then overdue. Anxious relatives awaiting the return of more than two hundred British passengers, demanded news. When it came, an elderly man collapsed, a young woman attacked the press with a stiletto-heel shoe and a man smashed press cameras. Mingled with the horror were elements of desperate hope, total incomprehension.

The worst disaster in air history left a trail of débris of all kinds scattered through the woods of the Ermenonville State Forest. The bric-a-brac of human lives is mingled with the remains of the crashed plane.

Overleaf: The doorway of the crashed DC10 of Turkish Airlines. Decompression resulting from the failure of the rear cargo door was revealed as the probable cause of the accident which killed 346 men, women and children.

Which of the London-bound passengers had transferred to the Turkish airliner? How could a plane, so fast, so safe and foolproof, just plunge to earth on a clear spring day? But it had.

The 'black box', which had automatically recorded all the aircraft's movements, was recovered intact, but it merely stated that the plane had reached 13,000 feet and then dived to a lower altitude before crashing – a fact already well-established. Ground controllers reported having heard a few seconds of excited, unintelligible speech before total silence when the DC10 left their radar screens. This suggested a disaster at 13,000 feet, and not an incomprehensible exercise in hedge-hopping.

The most popular theory was a bomb, but aircraft authorities were adamant that all passengers and luggage had been screened.

A fortnight later: the probable truth. Bodies had been found, still strapped in their seats, a full seven miles from the rest of the wreckage. Then the aircraft's rear cargo door was found, nine miles away, and this seemed to be the missing clue.

Two years before, in Canada, the faulty latch on a DC10 cargo door had nearly caused a similar tragedy. The door had opened suddenly in flight and this, for a reason which was not at first clear to the highly skilled crew, seemed to jam a number of the controls. Somehow they nursed it back to base.

The United States Federal Aviation Administration gave instructions for doors to be modified so that it was impossible for them to open in flight. Further recommendations were made to the manufacturer, McDonnell-Douglas of California, that the floor of the passenger compartment, immediately above the hold, should be strengthened and air vents made in it. This expensive modification would have to be for subsequent aircraft: meanwhile, the doors must be corrected; and McDonnell-Douglas passed on these comparatively simple instructions to all its customers.

Comparison with the near-disaster over Canada proved that the Turkish plane's cargo door had opened at 13,000 feet. This, as over Canada, had caused instant depressurization of the lower, cargo compartment. As in every section of a modern airliner, the cargo compartment was kept at an air pressure approximating to that on the ground; and when this pressure dropped suddenly the light passenger deck immediately above it collapsed. In the more serious Turkish case it dragged seats down into the hold, sucking a number of them in which occupants were still strapped out of the open doorway.

At this point the pilot might have been able to dive safely to a lower altitude – but the control cables of a DC10, from flight deck to tail, run under the passenger deck, and in the Turkish aircraft these were instantly and completely jammed. Helpless, the aircraft fell into a shallow dive which no pilot could have righted.

The recovered door showed that a vital flange, part of the safety modification, was missing. There was no doubt that it had been fitted but no certainty as to when it had come adrift. A cargo handler at Orly was for a time under suspicion of not having closed the door before take-off and furthermore of having been unable to read the instructions printed on it, but he and the airport authorities were able to dispel this suspicion.

Exactly a year later, a group of English people were taken to the scene by a French friend. The whole area had been enclosed by a high fence, and they had to be let in by the *Garde Forestiere*. They looked around them in horror at the wreckage, the minutiae of human tragedy, the bits of clothing, luggage and the rest. It would take years to retrieve all this, and the French government had decided the job should not be done by souvenir hunters, hence the enclosure.

'Yes', said the *Garde Forestière*, 'he might have made it, you know, that pilot from Turkey, he might have saved many lives because the place where he came down was fairly clear. But, *hélas*, he hit this rocky eminence here. And the plane simply broke up, wings, everything, going everywhere. That is why the felled bit of Ermonenville Forest is so large, why the fence has to be so long . . .'

Almost two years after the tragedy the first of many claims from dependents and relatives of those who died was settled in an American court. Others, of course, would follow. The sum awarded was large; as much punitive, some said, as compensatory – in order, perhaps, to impress upon all concerned that something of this sort should never, could never, happen again.

The huge aircraft ploughed a thousand-yard furrow through the trees of the woods in which it crashed, shearing them off short and starting a number of fires. The woods are a popular place for weekend strollers, but on that Sunday afternoon nobody on the ground was killed.

American Mid-West, 1974

For the people of the Gulf and Mid-western states of the U.S.A. the words 'Twister' holds terror. Even the sound of an approaching tornado is awesome; anyone unlucky enough to be in the direct path of a tornado without any shelter available has little chance of surviving it.

In April 1974, in the worst tornado disaster since 1925 (when nearly 700 people were killed), a total of 324 people became victims of tornadoes in the space of eight hours, and hundreds more were injured, while damage ran into many millions of dollars. Although warnings had been given, a part of the area which was struck in 1974 was unfamiliar with tornadoes, and this contributed to the high death-toll.

Nothing can be done to prevent tornadoes and little is known about them, although no storm is more violent. Unlike hurricanes, which can be observed from within, tornadoes are so small that their study has not been practical. The conditions which give rise to them, however, are well-known and are present when warm moist air-masses meet cold dry air-masses.

Precipitating the events of 2 and 3 April 1974 was the swift eastward movement of an egg-shaped mass of cool dry air about one thousand miles across, while at the centre of the air-mass was a region of low pressure similar to that found in the calm eye of a hurricane.

This low pressure region moved very fast from central Kansas to Iowa and then on to the northern tip of Michigan. In the northern hemisphere air circulates counter-clockwise, round a centre of high or low pressure. Winds to the east of the cool air-mass were moving north, and by 2 April this northward flow was carrying moist air from the Gulf of Mexico which was rapidly warming up with the coming of spring and evaporating large masses of water.

Meanwhile about 200 miles to the landward, westward edge of the air-mass a cold front, flowing off the Rocky Mountains, developed, and a series of squall-lanes (instability lines) were formed. There the moist air welled upwards rapidly, spurring a compensating downward flow of cooler air from above and the series of squall-lines brought tornadoes over Alabama, like 'jabs from a boxer' as a meteorologist described it.

Research shows that tornadoes arise within small cyclones, a few miles across, which in turn arise within large thunderstorms. In the funnel of a tornado winds may swirl at 300 miles an hour or more – four times as fast as those in a hurricane. The movement of a tornado has been likened to a dancer, pirouetting on a rotating platform which is itself mounted on a truck, and this accounts for the terrifyingly erratic and unpredictable route many tornadoes take. At the edge of the tornado-funnel trees are uprooted; in the centre, buildings explode and railway carriages are blown over. The twister may be only 100 feet across, but it can leave a trail of damage half a mile wide.

On these two days in April 100 twisters struck in the space of eight hours in an area from Alabama to Windsor, Ontario, across the Canadian border. Two of the worst hit towns were Xenia, Ohio, and Brandenburg, Kentucky, and neither town had much experience of the killing twisters; there had been only seven tornadoes in the Xenia area in the last 24 years, and no deaths, and Brandenburg had never experienced a tornado before.

Since tornadoes strike more than a thousand times a year in the United States, people living in the affected regions have learnt to take shelter when warnings are given; to leave their cars if they cannot drive clear of the twister's path and find some hollow, if they can, in which to hide; to keep away from windows which can shatter; to take cover under large pieces of furniture. In the worst areas the houses are built with storm cellars in which the occupants can take refuge.

In the late afternoon, against a sky filled with blackness and flying débris, one particular twister roared its way through Xenia from the south-west, slashing a path of destruction three or four miles long and several hundred yards wide. New housing developments, old neighbourhoods, schools, churches, downtown businesses and shopping centre, suffered equally. Within five minutes of sudden, shattering destruction 30 people died, nearly a hundred were injured, and thousands made homeless.

Left: This remarkable picture of a tornado shows its peculiar funnel-like form, and the huge dust cloud created by its erratic and terrifyingly destructive route. In the funnel of a tornado winds may swirl at 300 miles an hour.

been left before the twister had reduced everything round them to chaos.

At least half of Xenia had been destroyed and all the services disrupted. But by the next day the immense task of clearing up had already begun. Electricity was partly restored, and hundreds of volunteers came to help the population search for what remained of their possessions and to find some kind of shelter. A state of emergency was declared and national guardsmen – much of whose time was later spent in keeping sight-seers away – were ordered out in Xenia, in Louisville, Kentucky, and in similarly stricken towns throughout the states of Alabama, Ohio, Indiana and Tennessee. In these states people sifted through the splinters that had been their homes, scraped the débris from the streets and sawed up fallen trees. There was a strange calm as with 'serene faces and certain hands' – as one reporter described it – the volunteers cleared up the rubbish against a background of persistent siren wails.

Throughout the affected areas stories abounded of individual incidents such as that at Windsor, where the roof was ripped off the local curling rink, killing and injuring those in its path, while the bodies of those who had been inside were found scattered over the neigh-bouring fields; and the metal frame warehouse of a con-struction company in Fountaintown, Indiana, which was lifted off the ground and carried a mile.

Perhaps one of the saddest results of the tornado's vicious attack was the effect it had upon the 1,600 people living in Brandenburg, Kentucky, 32 miles west of Louisville. This small farming community sat on the banks of the Ohio River, and most of its inhabitants had lived there all their lives. It was a small society, intimate, chatty and with an air of permanence. Its local paper was small and gossipy, and everybody knew everybody and all about each other. Modest houses, mostly of nineteenth-century architecture, stood on top a pair of hills; the pace of life of Brandenburg was slow and restrained – it was 'a Mark Twain town'.

A few minutes of unleashed fury changed all this. Twenty-nine people died and scores were injured. Hundreds of people were made homeless as three-quarters of the buildings were damaged beyond repair. One 21-year-old girl and her 9-year-old brother were in a flat in an old two-storey house, clutching each other in terror as the tornado swept eastwards along the river's edge. Thirty seconds later they were trapped by wreckage while the neighbours in the flat downstairs – a woman and three young children – lay dead. The neighbour's infant daughter was found, in a field at the bottom of a hill 200 yards away, alive.

Later the river was dragged for bodies, as eye-witnesses spoke of houses, cars and bodies flying through the air. Such was the extent and importance of the destruction in this small community that many people decided to leave. It seemed pointless, they said, to try to rebuild: too much had gone for ever; the river town of Brandenburg had all but disappeared.

Months passed before the damage caused through-out the country could be repaired – it was estimated that damage to personal property alone had cost the country £1,000,000,000, and low-interest personal loans to home-owners and businessmen were immedi-ately announced. Damage to property can be made good, but nothing can replace a way of life.

Above : The damage of a tornado is devastating. In eight hours a series of 'twisters' rampaging through the American middle west killed 324 people, injured hundreds and caused damage such as that pictured here, which ran into many millions of dollars.

The people who had managed to take shelter emerged dazed, once the roaring inferno had passed, and took stock. They knew that the windows had shattered, for flying glass had rained upon them as they lay on the floors of the downstairs rooms, but out in the street they discovered that almost every house had lost its roof and many their first floors. Some were virtually heaps of rubble and splinters. Dangling wires, loose signs, branches, traffic-lights – all were strewn higgledy-piggledy across once orderly streets.

Cars had been tossed along the roads; a train passing through the town with a load of new cars was safe, but all the cars were dented and their glass broken. Débris littered the streets blown from miles away and among it, untouched by the wind – such is the caprice of torna-does – stood bizarre objects; a child's scooter, dressing-table ornaments, a pile of magazines, just as they had

Flixborough, 1974

In any disaster situation it is possible for the outside observer to look on the bright side and say that things might have been worse. Certainly with Britain's greatest industrial accident at Flixborough on 1 June 1974, things could have been a lot worse.

In the awesome explosion at the Nypro Works 29 people died and more than 100 were injured, while 100 homes in the village nearby were destroyed or badly damaged. People living 30 miles away thought there had been a nuclear attack, and one man in the Lincolnshire town of Scunthorpe, six miles away, said: 'It parted the clouds and went up like a mushroom – like an atomic bomb!' A village housewife declared: 'We thought they'd dropped an H-bomb. There was a mushroom-shaped cloud spiralling up with two great thick circles!'

The explosion happened at 4.53 p.m. on a Saturday afternoon when comparatively few people were about. Had it been a weekday the likelihood is that many of the 550 workers would have perished in the inferno which followed the explosion. The fire raged uncontrollably for 24 hours, and the Nypro factory was gutted.

Of the 29 who died there, 27 were employees, one was a sub-contractor, and one, an outside driver, happened to be in the wrong place at the wrong time.

The explosion occurred in the plant's Area One. A worker there, Lawrence Harry, said: 'We heard one bang followed by a huge explosion. Everything went pitch black and I was picked up and hurled 30 yards by the blast. For a while I was wandering about dazed, but then I found one of my mates was missing so I went back inside to try and find him.' In one of the laboratories a chemist technician, Tom McCale, saw the flash of the explosion and flames racing along a trail of leaking liquid gas. 'Let's get out of here quick!' he shouted to his seven companions, making for the door. They turned left, Tom turned right, and was engulfed in the force of the explosion. Seriously concussed, he was rushed to hospital.

A mile and a half to the south-west across the River Trent, in the village of Amcotts, Susan Dye's two children were playing out of doors. Nichola, aged three, and five-year-old Lisa were struck by glass splinters which embedded in their faces even before they heard the roar of the explosion. Mrs Dye gathered the screaming girls into her arms and hurried them to hospital. The doctors told her to hold them down on the operating-table as they removed the splinters and carefully stitched their wounds.

The blast took off slates and whole roofs in the village of Flixborough itself; all the windows were shattered, doors wrenched off and walls cracked. Chimney-pots came tumbling down into the streets and people were hurled about like rag-dolls. Within moments the peaceful scene resembled something out of the wartime blitz.

Of the 29 dead only eight bodies were recovered. The rest had been atomized by the force of the explosion and the savage blaze which followed.

The Flixborough Works was jointly owned by the National Coal Board and Holland's equivalent organization, the Dutch State Mining Company. It was the sole British source of caprolactam, an essential ingredient of nylon. The huge Dutch concern had developed the process for making a fibre they called 'Nylon 6' in the 1960s, and subsequently went into partnership with the British Coal Board. Flixborough supplied Courtaulds with 20,000 tons of caprolactam annually for their nylon goods manufacture, but with refinements in the operation they stepped this up to 70,000 tons by the mid-70s. The fibre went into the manufacture of goods ranging from ladies' tights and underwear to curtains, carpets, car-tyres and safety-belts, and Nypro supplied factories employing upwards of 30,000 workers. As a result of the explosion all these jobs were immediately threatened; with a temporary world shortage of caprolactam there was little chance of manufacturers being able to transfer their orders elsewhere.

If the surrounding villages thought they had witnessed an atomic explosion, the Courtauld company took the secondary shock-wave. As Nypro's biggest customer, £20 million was wiped off Courtaulds's stock-market value the following Monday.

Until Flixborough, modern industrial thinking had been to have a giant-scale operation to serve all the most useful purposes, rather than having many smaller plants dispersed about the country. The saving in transport and handling costs between subsidiary factories was a powerful argument; raw materials were cheaper to buy in bulk, and the hyper-factory located on one site often provided employment for virtually the entire local working population (although, curiously enough, not one of the 300 people in quiet, rural Flixborough worked at Nypro). After the explosion this view was called into question, for apart from the matter of having such an awesome explosive-packed complex within blast-distance of inhabited areas, the economic consequence of losing the entire basic raw material was self-evident.

British Employment Secretary Michael Foot set up a Court of Inquiry to establish the cause of the disaster. The government's Chief Inspector of Factories had warned in his 1972 report on modern high-technology factories: 'We are faced increasingly with the risk of failure which could result in multiple deaths and injuries of near-disaster proportions.' Many specialists in industrial safety methods had appreciated that in the event of such a failure it was vital that the right lessons should be learnt; that after any major disaster it should be possible to see where the shortcomings were in the chain of checks, tests, expertise and managerial control which determine the level of industrial safety in any British factory.

The year before the accident the Flixborough plant had begun using a speedier process of manufacture, a short-cut using benzene rather than cyclohexane to start the process. Benzene is cheaper, but also highly toxic, inflammable and explosive. After the benzene has been used to produce cyclohexane (a colourless liquid similar to petrol) this chemical is mixed with ammonia in an oxidizing plant. At this critical stage of the process the cyclohexane is under tremendous pressure and the oxygen supply must be precisely controlled. The result is cyclohexanone oxide, which is then treated with concentrated sulphuric acid or phosphoric acid at an isomerizing plant. This produces caprolactam, which in turn produces the fibre Nylon 6.

More than 1,000 tons of cyclohexane were stored at Flixborough in 1974, and the company stuck steadfastly to the safety and fire regulations. Workers were searched for lighters, matches and cigarettes, and in high-risk areas of the plant everyone had to wear special footwear; although, as it was pointed out at the inquiry, in certain circumstances if there was a gas leak on a warm day a man in a nylon shirt could create sufficient static electricity to cause a spark.

The inquiry delivered its findings in May 1975, nearly a year after the explosion, which it described as 'of warlike dimensions'.

On 27 March 1974, more than two months before the explosion, cyclohexane was found leaking from a six-foot crack in Reactor No. 5 in a linked series of six reactors. All six were closed down and company officials decided to remove Reactor No. 5 for inspection, and

Previous pages : Flixborough on fire.

Left : People were cut by flying glass seven miles away and the Nypro Works was reduced to a mass of twisted metal.

link Reactors 4 and 6 with a temporary bypass pipe. *This link was badly designed. Nobody consulted the relevant British Standards or the manufacturer's handbook which would have shown the link was unsafe.* The design staff were under pressure to complete their work so that production should be resumed. The emphasis was directed to getting the oxidation process on stream again with the minimum possible delay, though the inquiry accepted that the officials did not knowingly embark on a hazardous course.

The engineering staff at Flixborough was under strength. Both the managing director and the general works manager were qualified and experienced chemical engineers, but the position of works engineer was vacant. Said the report: 'There was no mechanical engineer on site with sufficient qualification, status or authority to deal with complex or novel engineering problems and insist on necessary precautions being taken.'

Before resuming production the five reactors and bypass pipe were pressurized with *nitrogen* to check that the system did not leak: the standard pressure test uses *water*, which is incompressible. If there is a leak, a rapid release of compressed nitrogen is itself dangerous. Had the correct tests been carried out they would almost certainly have shown the bypass pipe to be defective and the disaster would have been averted. From the end of March there had been no thorough inspection of the by-pass pipe.

In the early hours of 1 June pressure in the reactors built up unusually quickly. The increase in pressure was observed but its cause – almost certainly a high-pressure nitrogen leak into the system – was not. Production continued.

At 4.50 p.m. the bypass pipe burst, causing a cloud of cyclohexane to gather outside the reactor system. At 4.53 p.m. the cyclohexane exploded, and Nypro's £18 million Flixborough plant was quickly reduced to rubble. Blame had to be shared by many individuals both at board level and below, the report decided. Experts criticized the inquiry findings, claiming they were a whitewash of the chemical-process industry. Four independent witnesses supported a 'two-event' theory of the Flixborough disaster; that the rupture in the 20-inch temporary pipe was caused by a prior explosion in a permanent 8-inch pipe seconds before the big bang.

This was not merely a technical bicker. By blaming the 20-inch pipe, which everybody accepted was a slipshod piece of engineering, the report in effect gave hundreds of other chemical plants a clean bill of health. The implications of the 'two-event' theory are much more serious, for if the 8-inch permanent pipe *did* fail first it calls into question the design of other plants throughout the world.

Dr Tudor Jones of the University of Leicester supports the 'two-event' theory. In what must be one of the most extraordinary pieces of evidence ever presented to an inquiry, he said that the explosion was recorded in his laboratory on equipment plotting disturbances in the ionosphere, 100 miles up. Forty seconds before the main Flixborough shock his instruments had recorded another explosion, the equivalent of one ton of T.N.T. 'The two events are there, quite plain for everyone to see', he said. 'I think it is highly unlikely to be anything but a small "pre-explosion".'

Left : Flames continued to belch from the plant for hours.

Top : A victim surveys the damage. A hundred houses were wrecked in Flixborough.

Above : Eighteen hours later, firemen were still tackling the blaze. Twenty-nine people in the works died in the explosion on a Saturday afternoon, when most of the work force was absent.

Honduras, 1974

Until September 1974 Honduras was to most people only the name of a country, somewhere in Central America. An unparalleled disaster was to change all that, for by press, radio and television, the almost unknown became suddenly and dramatically familiar.

Honduras lies on the Caribbean in the north and the Pacific in the south and south-west, with Nicaragua to the east, Guatemala to the west and Salvador to the south. In extent it is slightly smaller than England, a country of mountains, deep valleys and fast-flowing rivers which flood down from the mountains to the coastal lowlands and thence to the sea. Essentially it is a very poor country. In 1870 vast sums of money were borrowed from London in order to build railways, but through incompetence and corruption most of the capital was dissipated and the country was left bankrupt and in a state of unrest. From 1883 until 1944 revolutions became a matter of course. No sooner had the Hondurans become familiar with one president than he was toppled from power and another, often very briefly, took his place.

Not that the majority of the country's some three million people have ever been interested in politics. For the most part they are of Indian stock, live in primitive conditions and are far too poor (£100 – or $250 – a year is considered a good wage) and far too busy trying to wring a meagre living from their small farms or farm-holdings to worry about what goes on in the Honduran capital of Tegucigalpa. Some breed cattle in the lowland pastures, but the country's chief product is bananas grown in large American-run plantations on the northern coastal plain and which, together with coffee, represents 50 per cent of the country's exports, the rest being made up of coconuts, timber and tobacco. It is a difficult country in which to travel because of a lack of good roads and railways and the deep valleys which cut through it like the troughs of waves (the Spanish word *honduras* may be translated as 'wavelike').

The country has two, or rather three, seasons – the wet from May to November, the dry from November to May, and September, the hurricane season. The terrible toll taken by hurricanes in the area nearly 8,000 people lost their lives in Haiti when Hurricane Flora struck in 1963) has led countries on the Atlantic and Pacific seaboards – especially the U.S.A. – to develop meteorological services with a multiplicity of weather stations, fleets of aircraft, banks of computers and all the other trappings of modern technology to monitor the atmospheric conditions which give rise to the violent disturbances from which hurricanes are created. When one such build-up was spotted in 1974, an urgent warning went to Tegucigalpa informing the government of Honduras that it was likely to be assaulted by a hurricane within the next 48 hours. Following the obscure system that bestows girls' names on hurricanes, this was given the somewhat frivolous name of 'Fifi'.

This house was washed up on top of a bridge in the Agwan Valley, near Tocoa by the severe floods which followed Hurricane Fifi.

The body of a child, one of 8,000 victims of Hurricane Fifi, lies at the edge of the Choloma River, four miles north of Choloma in northern Honduras.

Unfortunately, communications being what they were, little could be done in the outlying districts of Honduras. Those who were informed of the danger could only wait; those who were not – and that was the bulk of the population – went about their back-breaking task of scratching a miserable living from the soil, quite oblivious to the approaching menace.

Hurricane Fifi arrived at dead of night on Wednesday, 18 September, with winds of 140 miles an hour, and torrential rain. Two feet of rain fell in 36 hours. Although the hurricane winds caused the initial

damage, they soon passed and the subsequent fatalities were mainly the result of the flooding. The heavy rainfall caused the many rivers of Honduras to overflow from their sources high in the mountains right down to the plains. Dykes and banks disappeared into a maelström of swirling brown water, and almost everything that stood in the path of the floods as they roared down to the sea was swept away.

The poorly-built homes of the farmers and peasants – stone, wattle and clay for the most part – just disappeared. Even some of the sturdier houses were picked up and carried for several miles, and in some cases, when meeting an obstruction that even the roaring waters could not move, would be piled one on top of another.

Worst hit was the district around the town of Choloma, standing on the banks of the river which gave it its name. Flood water poured through the town bearing trees, rocks and pathetic jumbles of wreckage that had once been homes, carrying away every standing thing along the river's bank. During the first two terrible days more than 3,000 died in the town, many of the bodies never being recovered. Those inhabitants who were left were faced with another great hazard – cholera. Bodies lay everywhere, many half-buried in the nine-feet layer of mud that the floods had left. Soon, under the hot, tropical sun, decay began to set in. Soldiers were rushed to the area and were soon collecting the bodies, piling them into heaps for mass cremation, contrary to the Roman Catholic practice of burial. Nothing, not even the deep religious beliefs of four centuries, could stand in the way of priorities.

As they worked, scarves and handkerchiefs about their mouths to allay the dreadful odour of putrefaction, the pitiful survivors – about half the town's original population – stood and watched, helpless. Many, of course, had tragic stories to tell. 'People were very afraid to leave their homes,' said one survivor. 'I saw nine people from one family embrace each other; they were afraid to move. They died, holding each other in their arms.'

One old man who had lost his entire family in the flood went back to search the pile of wreckage that had been his home, and found the bodies of two dead people. He did not know them; they were not even people of Choloma. They were, as he remarked, 'just poor innocents who were swept down from the mountain and ended up here'. Another added that two separate floods had chased each other through the town early on the morning of Thursday, 19 September. 'The water poured across the street and between my home and my neighbour's like rapids.'

The second city of Honduras, San Pedro Sula, also took the full brunt of Hurricane Fifi and the floods which followed in her wake. With their homes wrecked or completely gone, some 400,000 people were suddenly homeless, without food and with the prospect of an epidemic very near.

The final death toll throughout the country was set at least at 8,000.

The first aircraft from neighbouring countries and the U.S.A. began to drone over the devastated areas, spotting thousands of terrified and desperately hungry survivors clinging to anything that protruded above the vast wastes of frothy, surging water. Some were soon saved, but the rescuers were unable to reach many of the rural areas of northern Honduras where thousands of peasants were marooned without food, fresh water or medical aid of any kind. To add to the difficulties, the only petrol refinery in the country had been isolated by the flooding of roads and the railway tracks, depriving the authorities of the fuel so vital for rescue work.

By 23 September helicopters from the U.S. base at the Panama Canal Zone were hovering wherever they could see signs of life, doubling their usual carrying capacity as they plucked wet, hungry and miserable survivors from roof-tops and trees. At first they were the only means of rescue, for bridges and railway tracks had been swept away and roads had disappeared beneath several feet of black, glutinous mud; electricity supplies were cut and telegraph-poles were down everywhere, while those that remained upright bore their pathetic bundles of squatting humanity whose upturned faces showed their mute appeal as the heavily-laden helicopters droned overhead.

As lines of communication were slowly restored, food and medical supplies began to arrive, Tocoa and San Pedro Sula becoming the main relief centres. Soon the stacks of supplies were beginning to grow, but the teams arriving from other countries ran into trouble. Corruption, always a major problem in any poor and under-developed country, became flagrant. Part of the Honduran army had been mustered to collect and distribute the food and other supplies; the rest was on guard along the Honduras/Salvador border and the government refused to bring them back and leave the border undefended. At the two main centres it was obvious that a large quantity of supplies was being diverted to a black market that had sprung into life within hours of the disaster.

Britain managed to bring some order out of the tension and even rioting at the centres. She had already sent in helicopters and troops with power-boats and medical teams from Belize in the then British Honduras, but realizing the problem was one of administration, co-ordinated all the endeavours of every assisting country through the newly-formed Whitehall Disaster Unit. This stamped out the corruption at source and helped the flow of rescue units, getting them with their supplies to the devastated areas where they were so urgently needed.

It was a prodigious task, for everywhere, it seemed, were thousands of starving people who had lost everything – corn, rice, beans and other subsistence crops having completely gone. For the country as a whole, things were even worse. With her economy utterly reliant on exports of bananas and coffee, and the plantations of these devastated, fresh crops had to be sown at once, with the prospect of at least two years wait before any return from the new plantings could be expected. Livestock had also perished in their thousands and these, too, would have to be replenished – although the country had no foreign currency available.

Only the generosity of other nations can enable Honduras to survive until she is able to return even to the near-starvation level that existed before Hurricane Fifi. Many peasants believe that the calamity was a punishment from God, but for what no-one is quite sure.

Darwin, 1974

Throughout Christmas Eve, 1974 local television and radio stations broadcast warnings of a cyclone, nicknamed Tracy, that was rapidly approaching Darwin, capital of Australia's Northern Territory.

The people of the city did not pay their usual heed to the continual warnings; they had Christmas preparations on their minds. This, surely, was no time to be unduly concerned about a cyclone which might easily miss the city entirely.

In the harbour the warning was acted upon almost immediately, perhaps because those on board the ships and boats had fewer distractions than people ashore, or perhaps they were inclined to be more weather-wise. The harbour began to empty during the early evening, 27 ships putting out to sea in order to ride out the cyclone. They, at any rate, were taking no chances. Three naval vessels, with their crews ashore, elected to stay.

As the evening wore on, the warnings became more insistent, and stated that the cyclone would pass right across the city some time around dawn, at 5.30 a.m. or so. But families, exhausted from last-minute shopping in the unusually humid weather and Christmas preparations, were in bed well before midnight. Soon the city was still.

At 1.30 a.m. on Christmas morning, the nightmare began; Tracy had arrived–four hours earlier than forecast. It arrived with a screeching, unbelievable wind that swept away everything that stood before it, accompanied by a full-throated roar that many later compared with a railway train emerging from a tunnel, but much, much louder.

The subsequent general impression was that the cyclone had 'struck like a bomb', and within minutes screaming residents ran into dark streets that suddenly had lost their comfortable, familiar look. Houses were torn from their foundations, and tall office buildings swayed and crumbled, cascading in utter ruins to lie in piles of masonry and timber. Parked cars were blown over; engines, carriages and trucks at the railway station were hurled about like toy trains; rails were torn from their sleepers and twisted into grotesque tangles of ironware. Telegraph-poles were swept away, wrapped around with strange bundles of twisted wires.

Tracy, its work done, passed over the city and, screaming and moaning as it went, faded away. There came a strange, sudden stillness, broken only by the occasional roar as a weakened building collapsed. A Qantas pilot flying over the city soon afterwards said: 'It was absolutely incredible. There was mile after mile of nothing but wreckage.'

All that remained of the once attractive city was a graveyard of devastation in which dazed inhabitants wandered as if stunned, or frenziedly scrabbled for relatives and friends beneath tons of rubble. Australia's deputy Prime Minister, Jim Cairns, was soon on the

scene and his first comment was that the destruction 'was quite unbelievable'. He went on to say: 'I had heard that Darwin was devastated, but I never imagined it could be as bad as this', stating that the damage was comparable to that caused by an atom bomb, for something like 90 per cent of the buildings in the city were shattered.

Announcing the news to a wider public Cairns stated: 'What happened to Darwin on Christmas Day has never happened in Australia before. Darwin is devastated. Darwin is destroyed. There is virtually no building in Darwin that is not severely damaged. Darwin looks like a battlefield or Hiroshima.'

Above: Tracy, the cyclone which was nature's Christmas gift to the citizens of Darwin, left this trail of destruction on either side of one of the city's main highways.

Above right: Tossed by the fierce vagaries of the 62 mile-an-

hour wind, a child's toy (above, right) lies beside overturned cars and damaged buildings. The destruction was 'unbelievable'.

Right : Fifty bodies were found in the ruins. Others may have died in boats which vanished from the harbour.

Of the small fleet of 27 ships that had moved out of the harbour into open water, only six returned under their own power. The rest had been hurled on to the rocks or had disappeared in a maelström of white, tortured water. Of the three naval vessels in the harbour, one had run aground, the other two had sunk. The harbour itself, as one observer said, looked like a 'junk-yard'. One ship had been picked up and blown 200 yards inland.

A graphic description of his personal ordeal came from skipper Bob Hedditch of the 73-foot prawn-trawler *Anson*. 'We put to sea on Christmas Eve at 19.30 hours and at midnight it hit us. The wind blew in our windows on the helm and tore off the back door. The waves crashed into the wheelhouse and I had to lie on the floor to steer. We had no steering by 0200 hours, no lights and only the main engine to keep us heading into the 162 mile an hour gale. We lost both our anchors and I didn't have a clue where we were. We saw two boats send up distress signals, but there was nothing we could do. We limped back at 1140 hours on the morning of Christmas Day.'

'It was our engineer's first trip to sea. He disappeared when we docked. I think it was his last trip, too!' Hedditch concluded wryly.

At Darwin airport, 50 planes were destroyed on the ground. Some were blown an incredible distance from where they had been standing. After doing his best to cope with the situation at the airport, John Auld, movement controller for Qantas, hastened to his car to drive home, concerned about his family who lived in one of the worst-devastated areas. He threaded his way past piles of rubble and wrecked cars, then decided to call briefly on his manager to give him an up to the minute report. When he arrived he found that his manager's house no longer existed – the site was entirely bare.

Deeply troubled, he drove to his own house. He found it a confusion of dust and débris, and no signs of his wife and child. After some frantic searching he found them in a neighbour's house. They had been discovered huddled together on the floor of the lavatory – the only room in the house which had not been wrecked – crouching there while the building seemed to disintegrate about them. Their escape was typical of the many that had occurred during that fateful night.

The complete death-toll has never been published. Although some 50 bodies were recovered, the actual figure could be much higher; many boats, for example, were not salvaged. The number of injured persons ran into hundreds.

Slowly and painfully the people of Darwin shook themselves free of the nightmare. The next day the Australian and world press reported the disaster, and relatives in other parts of Australia worried about the fate of their families. All telegraph-poles were down, but a temporary communications centre set up in Smith Street provided a free telegram or short telephone service for 'safe and well' messages. Queues for this formed for more than 200 yards.

As the catastrophe had ruptured water-pipes, a further centre was set up to provide water. Water-trucks were towed to a pipeline on Stuart Highway where, all modesty cast aside in the oppressively humid weather, men, women and children stood naked on the highway, revelling in the first shower they had experienced since the cyclone had struck.

Help was on the way. A fleet of seven ships, led by aircraft carrier H.M.A.S. *Melbourne*, was racing to the harbour, bearing emergency supplies. Fresh food and water was flown in daily. Arrangements were also put in hand for a massive airlift to take some 25,000 homeless people to other parts of the territory. By Sunday night, 29 December, more than 10,000 people had been airlifted – mostly the infirm, the ill and the young. As relief teams still toiled in tropic humidity, plans had already been put in hand for a new and even better Darwin.

It was estimated that about $250 million would be needed to replace the 10,000 or so homes that had been destroyed. Cairns had said that the catastrophe represented 'Australia's greatest national challenge for years and, typically, the people of Darwin were ready to meet that challenge.'

Eastern Airlines Boeing 727, Kennedy Airport, 1975

Doris Boehmann, secretary of the Cedarhurst Tennis Club near Brookville Boulevard, New York, had been looking forward to a busy day, with the courts and the club-room filled with members and their friends, playing and gossiping in the pleasant, relaxed atmosphere for which the Cedarhurst was famous. The previous day, however, the weather had changed and this Wednesday, 24 June 1975 was a bad one with constant rain, heavy clouds overhead and sudden gusts of wind.

She watched the airliners coming in to land at Kennedy, for the club-house was near the huge international airport. The great silver shapes roared overhead and then, flattening, each would touch down on the glistening runway. She was about to turn away when she heard the deep roar of another plane overhead. From its blue and white markings she knew that it belonged to Eastern Airlines. It was about 500 yards away from her, moving across the tennis courts and, as she reported later, far too low, 'about 40 or 50 feet off the ground'. As she watched there came a sudden flash of fire and then the aircraft began to break up in the air and fall, a tall pillar of black smoke rising from where it had crashed.

Others saw the disaster too, several claiming with much assurance that it had been struck by lightning just before it struck the ground. Paul Moran, a policeman, said: 'Lightning hit the plane and tilted it to the right. It went about 20 more yards and hit the ground.'

Another, Neal Rairden stated: 'I was about three blocks away when I saw the plane coming in. It was raining very hard at the time – about 4.10. All of a sudden there was lightning. I looked up and all I saw was smoke and flame and no plane. I said "Holy God!" I knew that plane had been hit by lightning.'

The aircraft was an Eastern Airlines Boeing 727 from New Orleans to Kennedy, carrying 116 passengers (including, as it was later discovered, a babe-in-arms not shown on the manifest) and a crew of eight. Among its passengers was a party of 19 Norwegian seamen from several ships in Louisiana port who were en route to their homeland for a holiday. They were among the first later to be identified, and some survived the disaster. One Egon Luftaas explained: 'The pilot seemed to go too much to the left, with one wing down. Then there was an explosion. Everyone was flung around. After that I can only remember the fire . . .'

In fact, the aircraft had not reached the airport but had crashed on the Rockaway Boulevard expressway on its north-eastern fringe in a relatively open section of Rosedale, Queens. It was the beginning of the rush hour, and many drivers had to brake frantically to avoid the burning wreckage that had been spilled out all over the road or to miss the other automobiles pulling up all around them – an especially hazardous procedure for the road was wet with rain and greasy with spilled fuel. The police were soon on the scene to be

met with lurid tales of how the crashing aircraft had smashed a number of cars off the road, but they were later able to report that not a single car had been hit.

The force of the impact as the plane struck the expressway sent a huge fireball into the sky and scattered bodies over a wide area. Fortunately there were few houses at this point, swampy ground being general on both sides of the road. Rescue attempts began almost immediately but they were seriously hampered by the dense traffic caused by the evening rush hour and by the thousands of sightseers who soon converged on the area. Initially rescuers were also delayed by the impossibility of getting into the fiercely burning fuselage to bring out any survivors. Many bodies were scattered on either side of the Rockaway Boulevard, on the boulevard itself and in an old garbage dump just beyond.

The massive emergency efforts that had been called into action by the disaster brought police and firemen, rescue crews and officials from the airport, and ambulances and helicopters racing to the scene, and the Jamaica and South Shore Hospitals in Queens and the Jacobi Hospital in the Bronx were alerted to receive the dead and injured. Kennedy Airport was closed a minute after the crash – at 4.11 p.m., the peak period of the day – and all air traffic was diverted until 4.53 p.m.

Rescue work went on under appalling conditions of darkness, incessant rain, a press of automobiles and gaping sightseers. One of the members of the first rescue team to arrive said, 'We got to the plane just as the first fire trucks were pulling in. Part of the fuselage and tail were on fire. We saw three survivors, two of them lying down and one walking up the road. You couldn't tell if it was a man or a woman. The person was all bloody. Somebody told the person to sit down and the first ambulance that came took the three away. What I was surprised about was that the other two didn't bleed as well.'

The first of the 19 City Fire Departments' equipment arrived and the firemen, wearing asbestos suits, had soon smothered the main fuselage with foam and the flames were quickly dowsed. The pitifully few survivors – 14 in all including two children – were rushed off to Jamaica Hospital where a large team of doctors, many of whom had dashed from their homes when the first news of the disaster came through on their radios, began the delicate task of treating excruciatingly painful burns.

The macabre task of collecting the bodies went on. They were gently laid down at the side of the road and covered with plastic sheets, some of which the rain soon moulded to pathetically small bodies of children. Somehow these shrouded bodies did not seem to be part of an aircraft disaster. There were just the formless mounds beneath the sheets with the scattered, personal objects that marked the whole as a tragedy involving *people* – a handbag, a shoe, a doll, a raincoat. A man's jacket was found lying in the garbage dump. In an inside pocket was more than $4,000, many in $100 bills, but with no indication of its owner. Nearby another jacket was found that had belonged to one of the Norwegian seamen. This also contained money, his pay-off and holiday money – $126.

At dawn the next day officials began to examine the whole disaster area in an endeavour to put forward an early explanation of the tragedy. It became obvious that the flight path of the aircraft had been disturbed by the turbulent weather, and that as it made its approach the plane had been sent out of control by the sudden and dreaded air currents known as 'shears'. It had been thrown to one side and had ploughed into the airport's approach lighting system. This consisted of strings of 20 groups of lights mounted on top of 30-foot metal towers each some 50 yards apart. The plane had obviously come in too low, missed the first two lights, struck the next two and then, missing the next as the pilot tried desperately to pull the plane's nose up, had swept on to demolish the next four, breaking up as it went. It finally plunged sideways and smashed on to the expressway, disintegrating into a thousand pieces that were strewn all over the road. Only two sizeable pieces of the aircraft remained, a large piece of the wing and rear section and part of the underside of the fuselage.

Inevitably, the question of the plane being struck by lightning, so definitely reported by several eyewitnesses, was raised, only to be rejected by the officials. One expert stated that if it was decided that the cause of the crash was due to lightning, it would prove to be a very rare case. 'Lightning strikes on aircraft are common, but seldom result in damage. Unless they are particularly severe they usually go unreported,' he said.

It was finally decided that what the eyewitnesses had thought to be lightning was probably electrical arcing caused when the plane had hit the high-intensity lights that marked the route to the runway.

Yet why had other aircraft which had arrived just before the Boeing 727 not similarly been affected? Three of these were a K.L.M. Boeing 747, a Flying Tiger DC8 and an Eastern Airlines L1011 Jumbo jet. Indeed, the pilot of the Jumbo, worrying about the vicious cross-winds that were throwing even his immense plane about in the air, diverted it to Newark International Airport after reporting such severe shifts that his inertial navigation system was indicating a stream of air moving at a speed of 60–80 knots.

The K.L.M. pilot stated that he found the speed of his aircraft suddenly dropped at 300 feet and he had quickly to boost the power to keep a level approach. He concluded with typically Dutch understatement: 'It was a very unstabilized approach.'

Curiously, the pilots of two other planes, a Finnair jetliner and a small private propellor plane reported that they had experienced no difficulty at all in landing.

The inquiry went on. The flight recorders and the cockpit voice readings were recovered intact, but revealed no indication from the control tower that an emergency was in operation. Kennedy Airport had the standard instrument landing system frequently used to guide aircraft down in bad weather and in any case, according to the control tower, there was only a six-knot wind, a 3,000-foot ceiling and five-mile visibility, conditions that would not normally trouble an experienced pilot.

What had caused the disaster? Was it the sudden air shift, the 'shears'? Had the pilot come too low and misjudged his altitude over the approach lights? Or did the one in several million chance happen, and had a bolt of lightning actually struck the aircraft?

Whatever the cause, the result was terrible – 110 persons killed. It was New York's worst air disaster in a decade and the second worst in the city's history.

Above : Towering monstrously over the bodies of its victims is the fuselage of the Boeing 727. Freak currents of air, lightning or human error—nobody can be sure what caused the crash.

Left : The crushed fuselage and at right the bodies of some of the 110 victims.

Guatemala, 1976

Relations between the Central American republic of Guatemala and the British Government had been tense for some time. The former claimed the neighbouring port of Belize in British Honduras, which had been settled by English buccaneers early in the seventeenth century and formally proclaimed a British possession in 1862. Indeed, during November 1975 the British Government, fearing an invasion, reinforced the garrison at Belize with men and aircraft, but this move appeared to aggravate the situation.

A conference was planned for the first week in February 1976 in an endeavour to arrive at some form of compromise for it was obvious that Guatemala would not readily yield her claim to what she felt was her territory by right, while the British government foresaw the introduction of a form of independence.

Preparations were in hand when, during the night of 4 February, Nature stepped in to postpone the meeting.

A tremendous earthquake struck Guatemala at 3.04 a.m., causing most of its population to pour out into the utter darkness of the night. Within the capital the blackness was lit garishly by sudden tongues of flame flaring upwards from shattered buildings, as in night attire and with blankets hastily draped across their shoulders, the panic-stricken people hurled themselves into the bitterly cold night air. The strident clangour of fire-engines and police vehicles effectively awoke the few who had slept through the initial thirty-second earthquake to the sound of the cries, moans and prayers of the thousands already thronging the streets.

Dawn revealed utter chaos. At least one-third of the buildings of the capital, a city of 1,000,000 people, had been destroyed; there was no water, no electricity and, at first, no organization. It was left to relatives and neighbours to dig frantically among piles of rubble in the hope of finding survivors. Yet even as they scrabbled with spades, broken timber and their bare hands, continual tremors still shook the city, bringing down loosened masonry and starting fresh fires. Altogether some 20 strong tremors were experienced on the first day.

Communication with the outside world was limited to contact by radio. In America, however, the possible extent of the damage was realized even before it was known by the Guatemalan authorities, for at Boulder, Colorado, the seismological station had recorded the earthquake, placing its epicentre at some 120 miles from the capital and measuring an ominous 7.2 on the Richter scale.

Later that day Colonel Manuel Ponce, the military chief of staff of the Guatemalan National Emergency Committee, called a news meeting of officials and pressmen. He announced that at least 2,000 people had been killed throughout the country and insisted that this figure, disturbing as it was, was 'conservative' and that, even as he spoke, alarming reports were coming

in from the interior. Teams of rescue workers were desperately trying to reach towns and villages that had been devastated to the north and east of the city, thousands of survivors were without food, medicine or even drinking water, and thousands of injured – many seriously – awaited the arrival of help of any kind.

As those who had attended this sombre meeting walked out on to the dark streets, crimson flames were thrusting skywards from the Guatemala University's new pharmaceutical school and from an international food institute nearby. The unlit streets were still crowded with people who preferred to face the chill of the night and a near-freezing temperature rather than risk being trapped under masonry, should another serious shock occur. Guests at the expensive tourist hotels in the central area of the capital were preparing to spend the night on the floor near the hotel entrances for fear of being trapped and crushed beneath the débris of already badly shattered buildings.

On the morning of Thursday, 5 February long queues formed outside shuttered shops in the vain hope of buying food, but few opened that day. Most of the city was without drinking water, although electricity had been restored to the central area. One of the hardest hit sections in the city was the slum district where most of the shanty buildings had collapsed at

Above : Destruction and damage to buildings where a disaster has occurred is easily depicted. Human tragedy is not so easy to capture, but it is in this that the real disaster lies. In the village of San Pedro some 300 people died. As the sun rises residents carry their dead from the church in the background towards the cemetery.

Right : In Guatemala City a woman watches anxiously as a doctor treats her injured baby. A total of 23,000 people died in Guatemala.

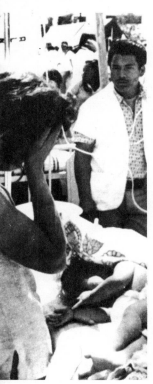

the first shock. The unfortunate inhabitants were now living under improvised shelters of sheets, table-cloths and scavenged pieces of corrugated iron, which offered poor shelter for such cold nights. The city was placed under a state of emergency, with troops patrolling the streets and manning machine-gun posts erected at strategic corners.

On learning of the disaster, the Governor of Belize immediately offered to fly in helicopters to help lift the injured and to provide other assistance. His offer was refused by the Guatemalan authorities. The British Government also offered to send any aid that was needed and British Airways volunteered to provide free cargo space for relief supplies, but the offer was firmly declined, although with consummate tact. A Guatemalan spokesman replied: 'Thank you very much. I am sincerely grateful. It is very thoughtful on the part of the British Government but just now we do not require it.'

By this time the magnitude of the disaster was fully appreciated and alleviation of the situation to meet the urgent needs of the victims came under the direction of the United Nations disaster relief co-ordinator. The League of Red Cross Societies launched a world-wide appeal for funds. In London, the British Red Cross and Help the Aged each announced an immediate donation of £5,000 ($10,000) to the victims of the earthquake. On the day after the earthquake, a team of United States Army disaster relief experts flew in from the Panama Canal Zone and CARE, the American relief organization, began to airlift many tons of food.

The night of 5 February saw most of the population again huddled together in the open. Although many were forced into this because they lacked any shelter, many more were influenced by memories of a similar disaster in their country in 1917, when the first major earthquake had been followed by another and far more fatal shock a week later.

Such forebodings were realized on 6 February when two strong tremors again rocked Guatemala city. They were part of the aftershock, and registered 5.75 on the Richter scale, slightly less than the original earthquake two days earlier. Two hours elapsed between each, the second being followed by a series of smaller tremors. They occurred while firemen were digging among the rubble that had resulted from Wednesday's earthquake. By then the Guatemalan National Emergency Committee had announced provisional figures of 5,000 dead and 15,000 injured.

Hunger, and especially thirst, were causing great suffering in Guatemala City and, indeed, in every town and village in the country. In the capital and larger towns, looting and violence increased and five people were executed in Guatemala City, where army patrols had been brought in to prevent the city from lapsing into chaos. The authorities issued constant appeals for order and calm, but there were frequent fights at emergency food centres and many instances of looting from devastated shops, an understandable crime when families are starving and the sight of easily obtainable food proves more powerful than moral codes.

News soon arrived of the state of the outlying areas, especially to the north-east, the epicentre of the earthquake. In the town of Joyabax, for example, some 55 miles from the capital, hardly a building was left standing and much of the town was under six feet of rubble, from which more than 500 bodies were recovered.

By 8 February, René Baralt, senior relief officer, announced that the death-toll could well rise to 20,000, for the casualty lists had already reported over 12,000 dead and 30,000 injured. Later figures placed the number of dead at 23,000. The Guatemalan earthquake was the worst since 1970, when 50,000 people had died in northern Peru; it was the second worst disaster in the Western hemisphere in modern times.

The donations continued to pour in. In Britain, Christian Aid and Oxfam each subscribed another £5,000 ($9,500) and the Catholic Fund for Overseas Development gave £2,000 ($3,800); Christian Aid later sent a further £20,000 ($40,000). Over £60,000 ($114,000) was spent in Britain on tents, blankets, medical supplies and a sanitation unit. The cost of the transportation of these supplies was taken over by voluntary agencies because of Guatemala's refusal to accept official help from Britain. Even so, permission was withheld for an aircraft flying from Gatwick to land at Guatemala Airport and the plane had to fly on to the neighbouring country of El Salvador, to be unloaded there and the urgently needed relief supplies then transported overland to the disaster areas. Thanks to the response to the call for vaccine, the ever-present fear of a major epidemic was averted.

America sent in 20 Air Force helicopters and their pilots returned with frightening reports of the devastation in the highland areas, where Indian groups lived in hundreds of small, scattered settlements, many of which were not even shown on local maps. First reports estimated that at least 80 per cent of their flimsy dwellings had been destroyed and that the people were in terrible straits, suffering from lack of water and food.

During the evening of Monday, 9 February, James Cameron made an appeal for financial help on British television and on the following day, Jorde Rosales, a Guatemalan doctor working for Save the Children Fund cabled to that organization's London headquarters: 'Desperately in need of vaccines – tetanus, typhoid and polio – and food of high calorific value. Also need refrigerators to keep vaccines fresh.'

On 10 February, Guatemala's President Kjell Eugenio Langerud announced that 17,032 had died, 54,826 had been injured and 221,994 people made homeless. These figures could hardly have been exact because even as he spoke, relief workers were struggling to reach devastated villages in the northern highlands where they pulled corpses from the wreckage of what once had been their homes. Makeshift landing strips were hacked out of scrub and bush to enable doctors and other relief specialists to fly in to the Indian settlements to airlift the wounded. All the hospital beds in Guatemala City were already filled and the injured were placed in the buildings of a trade fair or taken to an American field hospital set up at Chimaltenango, 40 miles north-west of the capital.

Thanks to the response to the call for vaccine the ever-present fear of a major epidemic was averted.

The magnitude of the disaster ruled out proper burial. Instead, communal graves were dug to receive the pitiful remains of thousands of victims, some in properly constructed coffins and then, as supplies ran out, in makeshift enclosures.

Index

The publishers would like to thank the following individuals and organizations for their kind permission to reproduce the photographs in this book:

Associated Press Ltd: 14, 15, 49, 50-51, 50 below, 51, 54-55, 56 above, 70 below, 74 above, 88-89, 91 above right, 101 above, 103 above, 112-113 below, 114-115 above, 114-115 below, 118 below, 121 below; Barnaby's Picture Library: 16-17, 21; Camera Press Ltd: 8, 26 above left, 68-69, 71 below, 76, 84-85, 86 above, 87 below, 95 above, 95 below, 98, 99 above, 110-111; Cine Foto Bucci: 52, 53; Daily Telegraph Colour Library: 87 below; R.A.Gardner: 12, 13; John Hillelson Agency Ltd: 96-97, 101 below, 102, 103 below; Illustrated London News: 18 below, 24 below, 24-25 above, 27, 28-29, 29, 33 below, 34-35, 36 below, 40 above, 42, 44 above, 44 below, 45 above; Keystone Press Agency: 46-47, 57 above, 57 below, 64-65, 66-67 above, 67 left, 77 below left, 77 above right, 82, 83 above, 88, 91 above left, 91 below, 113 below; London Express News and Feature Services: 80-81, 81, 100, 116-117, 117 above, 117 below; Mansell Collection: 19 below; Mirror Group Newspapers Ltd: 22-23; Photri: endpapers, 5, 36-37 above, 37 below, 104, 104-105, Peruvian Embassy: 94; Picturepoint Ltd: 83 below, 99 below; Popperfoto: 40 centre left, 40-41 below, 41 above, 45 below, 67 right, 70 above, 71 above, 72, 72-73, 74-75, 75, 78 above, 78 below, 79, 90, 92, 93, 118-119, 120-121; Press Association: 38 above; Radio Times Hulton Picture Library: 11, 17, 18-19 above, 20, 24 above centre, 24 above left, 25 right, 32 above, 32 below, 33 above, 36 centre, 37 centre, 39, 43; Rapho (Bajande): 106-107, 109, (S. Duboy): 6-7, 108; Sungravure Syndication: 60-61, 62, 63 above, 63 below; Syndication International: 26 below right, 30 above, 30 below, 31 above, 31 below, 38 below, 48, 56 below, 86 below, 112 above, 113 above; Wilson and Horton, New Zealand: 58, 59 above, 59 below.

Back Jacket: Radio Times Hulton Picture
              Library.

PDO 82-1143